What professionals are sa

RESILIENT CHILDREN

"Throughout my twenty-eight years of practice as a psychiatrist, I have believed in the concept of primary prevention, which is the prevention of illness and not simply the treatment of it. *Resilient Children* provides the principles, strategies and techniques to help children to develop the necessary strengths and skills to thrive in a dynamic world filled with opportunities and challenges. This manual is a phenomenal resource for those who teach and work with children. It will undoubtedly have a lasting impact for our children and the resilience of our communities."

Laurence E. Jackson, M.D., Psychiatrist

"*Resilient Children* provides creative, age-appropriate learning opportunities for young people to develop personal skills for handling life's challenges in a positive and productive manner. The lessons may be used by teachers to supplement state-adopted standards for health education. Each activity is designed to promote individual and cooperative learning. Opportunities are also provided for critical thinking and problem solving that focus on personal responsibility. In addition to classroom use, materials are also suitable for parents, grandparents, and/or therapists to use one-on-one."

Barbra Johnson, M.A., School Administrator

"I commend whole-heartedly your work to help children to develop a healthy and wholesome sense of self with a high degree of resiliency for the life situations they can encounter. The tools you have developed will be a great asset to parents, teachers and other adults to assist children when they are struggling."

William F. Condon, Pastor

"The activities in *Resilient Children* are enlightening and impactful, and I have successfully used them in my classroom to supplement my curriculum for developing independent thinkers. The versatile and imaginative activities are easily adapted to individual needs and lend themselves to the many flexibilities that a classroom may require."

Marsha Korkowski, M.A., Elementary School Teacher

"A practical resource where kids can get the social-emotional skills to navigate their lives positioned for success."

Thomas McEuen, Ph.D., Psychologist

"These are wonderful, creative suggestions to use in sessions with individual children or groups. I'm excited to have *Resilient Children* as a new resource."

Rebecca Hurst, L.C.S.W., Licensed Clinical Social Worker

RESILIENT CHILDREN

How caring adults can inspire children to succeed and thrive

Pam Farkas, L.C.S.W., Jerry Binder, Ph.D., Barrie Richter, B.A.

ISBN: 978-1-60594-695-5 (PB)

Library of Congress Control Number: 2011901924

This book is designed to provide information and be used in regard to the subject

matter that is covered. It is informational and educational, and is not intended to

take the place of professional services. Where there are concerns, a competent professional

should be consulted.

The authors have provided an online extension to complement the ideas and materials in

Resilient Children, www.resilientchildren.info. The online companion to this work provides

downloadable lessons, blogs, suggestions and commentary from parents and professionals

and additional resources on developing resiliency in children.

Inquiries about this book should be addressed to the authors at:

Dr. Jordan M. Farkas Foundation

8415 Coreyell Place

Los Angeles, CA 90046

www.resilientchildren.info

Dedication

Past, Present and Future

With much love to Jordan, who lived a vibrant and thoughtful life even while struggling with depression. He is dearly remembered for his amazing smile, clever wit and boundless curiosity. His broad intellect and his notions of justice drove his need to always speak out. He brought joy and comfort to many people during his lifetime, and his family and friends will always remember him.

To Joel and Liat, who live with optimism and love, valiantly meeting challenges and embracing the gifts of family, meaningful work and fulfilling relationships.

To Ethan and Eliana, who are blessed with health and vibrancy. May they fulfill their hopes and dreams.

CONTENTS

INTRODUCTION

Are you among the many caring adults who fulfill an important role in a child's life?

Are you a parent, teacher, grandparent, home school teacher, foster parent, camp counselor, uncle, aunt, clergy, mentor, psychotherapist, coach, family friend, or social worker?

If so, RESILIENT CHILDREN is a valuable resource for you to use to empower and fortify children. It provides them with positive choices for navigating everyday life challenges competently and successfully.

RESILIENT CHILDREN is a resource of skill building lessons for children, from kindergarten through grade six, ages 5 – 12, to help them to succeed and thrive. Here, you will find the vital fundamental knowledge, attitudes and skills that are the essential building blocks of resiliency.

RESILIENT CHILDREN is based on research that resiliency skills can be learned and developed. The skills are introduced at kindergarten age, and as the children grow and mature, the concepts and learning activities expand to match their intellectual and emotional levels.

What is RESILIENCY?

Resiliency is the ability to overcome adversity and to bounce back in the face of difficulty, challenge and stress. Resiliency is a positive outlook and approach to life. It contributes to building durable social and emotional health. Researchers agree that the inborn capacity for resilience is present from early childhood.

Just like adults, children have to cope with unexpected problems and difficulties. Some of these life stressors could be from poverty, family turmoil, divorce, abuse, homelessness, chronic illness or bullying. Or it could simply be trying to make a new friend, solve a problem, or express feelings. If children do not develop effective resiliency skills they are more at risk for being overwhelmed, becoming isolated and withdrawn, turning to drugs and alcohol or other high-risk or self-abusing behaviors, underachieving in school, becoming depressed and even more likely to be thinking of suicide.

Think of resiliency as a set of "protective factors" which can counter the "risk factors" that negatively impact a child's life. It's an inoculation against whatever threatens a child's personal growth and well-being. Resiliency builds over time and promotes the unfolding of competency, self-confidence and optimism.

The four A's of resiliency are: **attitude**—a secure sense of self, embodied in ideas and belief; **ability**—a repertoire of skills that are developed and strengthened; **achievement**—a rewarding sense of personal accomplishment; **affect**—the pleasurable emotions of well-being, confidence and security that accompany contending successfully with everyday life challenges.

Resilient adults have a "tool box" of personal strengths and skills to fortify them against the hassles and difficulties of daily life. Children, though more vulnerable to adversity, can also learn fortifying and protective resiliency skills. How? Developing resiliency is similar to developing physical fitness. Children can exercise their minds to achieve resiliency just as they can exercise their bodies to achieve physical fitness. Over time, with repetition and reinforcement, the skills become integrated into the child's "tool box" of personal strengths.

ATTITUDE

ABILITY

AFFECT

ACHIEVEMENT

The school is among the many places in our society where children learn how to make smart choices and take responsibility for their own social-emotional health and well-being. School programs are teaching children effective decision-making and positive refusal behavior to combat negative influences.

Schools, however, are not the only places where children can learn how to cope with everyday life. Daycare centers, home schools, counseling sessions, religious or community organizations, homeless shelters, clubs, athletic playing fields and camps also play crucial roles in the lives of children. Adults in trusting relationships with children in these various settings can convey the essential knowledge, attitudes, and skills that are the fundamental building blocks of resiliency. In these places, children need to feel safe to express their emotions, concerns and hopes without fear of being judged.

If you're a parent, family member or caring adult, these learning activities can be done informally at home, in a park, or wherever you choose. If you're a psychotherapist or social worker, these learning activities can be the basis of a session for skill building or behavioral rehearsal. They can easily be incorporated into play therapy or a family therapy session. For teachers, these learning activities can be an entire curriculum or used as needed when situations arise. Coaches and mentors can use them in specific-need situations.

Resilient Children embraces the many different ways that children learn—verbally, artistically, physically, visually and musically. The activities are structured for either individual or group learning, and they can be tailored in any way that better meets the needs of these children. The resiliency skills can be used in any order. If a child seems to have difficulty making friends, then start with Friendship Skills. If a child is being bullied, then you would want to begin with Anti-Bullying Skills.

Though the concepts and applications of resiliency described in these pages are based on research, keep in mind that they are about children in general and may not be appropriate where there are special concerns. In such situations, professional assistance may be required.

Right now, children need the nurturing and mentoring of caring adults who can teach them social-emotional skills, not just for coping, but for succeeding and thriving throughout their life. *Resilient Children* provides these essential lessons. This book will provide what every caring adult needs to inspire children to become their best.

Six Skills of RESILIENCY

1. SELF-AWARENESS SKILLS

Self-awareness skills are about developing a "response-ability" to feelings, beliefs, values, hopes and strengths. Self-awareness teaches children that they are unique in how they grow, learn and thrive, and at the same time how they share similarities with others. This awareness of self is essential for developing self-respect, self-esteem and self-confidence; it extends beyond the self, to the family, community and society. Also, robust self-awareness is a protective factor against many of the negative forces that can undermine a child's life and lead to underachievement, frustration, or self-harming behaviors.

2. EMOTIONAL SKILLS

Emotional development includes the skills of recognizing and expressing emotions and developing a vocabulary of feeling words. These skills are integral to the complex processes of socialization, enriching individual identity and promoting self-esteem. Children learn that feelings are natural, and are neither right nor wrong. Learning how to manage disturbing or harsh emotions is an additional skill learned through role-playing and behavioral rehearsal. Taken together, these skills are additional building blocks of resiliency.

3. COMMUNICATION SKILLS

Communication skills are indispensable in everyday life. Far more than the exchange of words, communication includes the tone and quality of voice, eye contact, body language and listening. Sometimes communicating is asking for help in situations that involve health, safety and saving a life. could be at school, on a street, in a park, or in a child's home. As communication skills develop, resiliency is strengthened, and a child is increasingly more adept at handling life situations.

4. CONFLICT SOLUTION SKILLS

Solving conflict situations peacefully and cooperatively builds self-confidence and the ability to manage differences verbally rather than by hurtful actions. Some specific positive skills that children can learn for solving conflicts are cooperation, empathy, appreciating differences, active listening, and impulse control. When it comes to interactions with others, knowing how to de-escalate conflict situations empowers children. These skills are essential for developing resiliency.

5. ANTI-BULLYING SKILLS

Resisting bullying is a resiliency skill. *Resilient Children* presents opportunities for learning and practicing skills for resistance to an array of bullying behaviors—harassment, physical intimidation and verbal threats. This book provides a framework for children to identify the differences between bullying and teasing and to develop appropriate responses to such behaviors. These learning activities help children focus on the boundaries between appropriate playful and inappropriate hurtful behavior.

6. FRIENDSHIP SKILLS

A resilient child is well liked by peers, is emotionally adjusted, and less inclined to engage in aggressive behaviors. Thus, learning effective friendship skills are fundamental for social and emotional development. Helping children develop and keep rewarding relationships is a critical aspect of friendship building. *Resilient Children* teaches children the skills of how to interact with others, how to value friendships, and what expectations to have about friends.

How To Use **RESILIENT CHILDREN**

Resilient Children is divided into three separate groupings by grade and age: grades K-2 (ages 5-7); grades 3-4 (ages 8-9); grades 5-6 (ages 10-12). Six fundamental resiliency skills are presented at the appropriate intelectual, emotional and social level for each grouping. For each skill there are several exercises which can be done one-on-one, in pairs, or as a small or large group. Remember, ability level is unique and complex. A child may not always proceed in the same steps at the same time and same way as others. Be positive and encouraging, and be sure to validate individual differences and achievements.

Each skill building lesson has five sections. To ensure success, read through all five sections of a lesson completely before beginning any instruction.

These are the sections:

1. **Main Idea** states the essential concept that is being taught.

2. **Teaching Points** support and elaborate on the Main Idea.

3. **Materials** are the items needed to complete the learning activity.

4. **Learning Activity** is the actual experience in which the child or children will participate.

5. **Discussion** includes questions to promote insight and reinforcement from the learning activity.

How Children Develop And Learn
Ages 5 - 7

Beginning school introduces children to a larger world of new experiences. In this age range they enjoy learning through imaginative games in small groups. A favorite is "Let's Play Make Believe." They also learn well from stories. They can be helped to handle their feelings if they are given the words. They are also inclined to compare themselves to others in terms of size, learning ability and appearance, and will leave a family or friend's game if they feel inferior. Five year old children fear the unfamiliar. Emphasize that they will be safe trying these new learning activities with you. At six, they typically enjoy a structured activity, so be sure to stay "on task." Expect a longer attention span and more questions from seven year old children and more advanced art projects owing to a growing familiarity and mastery of different materials. Language usage in this age range means that children's vocabulary is growing and self-expression in writing is increasing. They are also deepening their empathy and their ability to comprehend the actions and feelings of other girls and boys. Their friendships are beginning to be more important as they evolve a growing independence from family. This is a crucial time to be building confidence in all areas of life, such as through friends, schoolwork and sports. Physical, social and thinking skills are also developing.

Ages 8 - 10

Children in this age range are becoming more adept at working independently at creative solutions to problems. They have a stronger sense of right and wrong. Because they possess more highly developed thinking skills, they are better able to draw meaning from stories that convey a message. Their attention span is lengthening and their vocabulary is growing. They now perceive a sense of self-worth more strongly and express it in many different ways. Yet, they may show frustration more visibly at what they are unable to do. Children in this age group tend to think of themselves in higher abstract concepts such as "I am smart in math." At the same time this is the age where a child is learning to conceal emotions from peers. Learning how to manage and express emotions is crucial during these years. Children develop this ability through experiences with parents and peers—and in many of the learning activities in *Resilient Children*. By age ten children demand more of their friends. Friendships become more intense as kids grow older. Both boys and girls want best friends, and by age ten most children do know how to be a good friend.

Ages 10 - 12

Children's ever-increasing independence from the family and their stronger bonding with friends and peers is more obvious at this age. It becomes more emotionally important to have healthy friendships, especially of the same gender. They are well aware of the opinions, judgements and accomplishments of their peers. Peer pressure can become intense during this time. Children who feel good about themselves are more able to resist negative peer pressure and make better choices for themselves. This is an important time for them to gain a sense of responsibility along with their growing independence. There is more of a sense of social conscience and empathy. There is a desire to conform and not stand out, yet to be aware of what makes them unique. Children at this age may begin to have feelings of insecurity, self-doubt and lack of self-confidence so we teach self-awareness to fortify self concept. By this age, eleven-twelve year old children have also acquired a greater knowledge base. They begin to see parents and authority figures as fallible human beings. They may even outwardly disparage or defy adult authority.

GRADES K-2 (AGES 5-7) LESSONS

RESILIENCY 1: SELF-AWARENESS SKILLS (K-2)

MYSTERY GRAB BAG

MAIN IDEA

Self-awareness is recognizing and appreciating how each of us is unique and special. This includes our personal qualities and skills, and the ways in which we grow, learn and thrive. At the same time, we learn to appreciate and respect what is distinct and similar about others. With a healthy foundation of self-awareness, resiliency can develop and grow.

TEACHING POINTS

★ We are all unique.

★ We share similarities with others.

★ We can learn to appreciate how each of us is unique yet similar.

MATERIALS

★ 6" x 8" blank index cards

★ markers and pencils

★ a large paper bag labeled *Mystery Grab Bag*

LEARNING ACTIVITY: *Mystery Grab Bag*

1. Hand out materials. Help children to write their first names on one side of their cards. Have them turn over the cards and draw a picture of something about themselves, such as a skill or a sport at which they excel.

2. Collect the cards and place them in the *Mystery Grab Bag*. Shake up the bag.
Next, remove one card at a time and show the picture side. Invite the children to guess whose card it is. Play for 10-15 minutes.

DISCUSSION

1. What was it about each picture that helped you know who it was?

2. Were some drawings similar? In what ways? What does that tell us?

3. How are some pictures different from one another?

4. How is each person special?

5. Why is it important to feel good about what makes you unique and similar?

RESILIENCY I: SELF-AWARENESS SKILLS (K-2)

UNIQUE AND SIMILAR

MAIN IDEA

Self-awareness is recognizing and appreciating how each of us is unique and special. This includes our personal qualities and skills, and the ways in which we grow, learn and thrive. At the same time, we learn to appreciate and respect what is distinct and similar about others. With a healthy foundation of self-awareness, resiliency can develop and grow.

TEACHING POINTS

★ We are all unique.

★ We share similarities with others.

★ We can learn to appreciate how each of us is unique yet similar.

MATERIALS

★ *Unique and Similar* activity sheet

LEARNING ACTIVITY: *Unique and Similar*

1. Ask the children to pair up with partners.

2. Hand out the *Unique and Similar* activity sheet.

3. Ask them to look at one another and find three ways that each of them is unique and three ways that each of them is similar. Write these down on the activity sheet. Have them share what they have written.

DISCUSSION

1. How is each of us unique?

2. How are we similar?

Name_____ Date_____

RESILIENCY 1: SELF-AWARENESS SKILLS (K-2)

UNIQUE AND SIMILAR

A PICTURE OF ME	A PICTURE OF MY PARTNER

WAYS MY PARTNER AND I ARE UNIQUE:

1. _____

2. _____

3. _____

WAYS MY PARTNER AND I ARE SIMILAR:

1. _____

2. _____

3. _____

RESILIENCY 1: SELF-AWARENESS SKILLS (K-2)

MIRROR, MIRROR

MAIN IDEA

Self-awareness is recognizing and appreciating how each of us is unique and special. This includes our personal qualities and skills, and the ways in which we grow, learn and thrive. At the same time, we learn to appreciate and respect what is distinct and similar about others. With a healthy foundation of self-awareness, resiliency can develop and grow.

TEACHING POINTS

★ We are all unique.

★ We share similarities with others.

★ We can learn to appreciate how each of us is unique yet similar.

MATERIALS

★ mirror

★ drawing materials

★ paper

LEARNING ACTIVITY: *Mirror, Mirror*

1. Hand out the mirror, paper and drawing materials. Have the children look in the mirror and see the special features of their faces. Take the children on a "guided tour" of their faces, feature by feature. Use affirming language for their hair, foreheads, eyebrows, eyes, mouths, skin, ears, chins and necks.

2. Use the mirror as an aid to have the children draw pictures of their faces. Encourage them to include all their special features. Display their pictures.

DISCUSSION

1. If I need to send someone to look for you, how would I describe your face?

2. What features do you like best about your face?

RESILIENCY 1: SELF-AWARENESS SKILLS (K-2)

I AM GREAT

MAIN IDEA

Self-awareness is recognizing and appreciating how each of us is unique and special. This includes our personal qualities and skills, and the ways in which we grow, learn and thrive. At the same time, we learn to appreciate and respect what is distinct and similar about others. With a healthy foundation of self-awareness, resiliency can develop and grow.

TEACHING POINTS

★ It's who I am, not what I do, that makes me great.

MATERIALS

★ chalkboard, whiteboard or chart paper

LEARNING ACTIVITY: *I Am Great*

1. Tell the children that they are going to talk about a subject that they know well—themselves! Ask them to think about some of their many wonderful qualities.

2. On the board, write down a child's name and ask that child to tell you one of his special qualities. Suggest examples: "I am always on time." Or "I am a good friend." Or "I tell the truth." Continue listing other children's names and their qualities on the board.

3. Next, call out each child's name that's on the board and invite others to name another special quality about that child.

DISCUSSION

1. How does it feel to say positive things about yourself? About others?

2. Were you suprised to hear others name a quality that you didn't think you had?

3. Why is it important to know your own special qualities and those of others?

PEOPLE

MAIN IDEA

Self-awareness is recognizing and appreciating how each of us is unique and special. This includes our personal qualities and skills, and the ways in which we grow, learn and thrive. At the same time, we learn to appreciate and respect what is distinct and similar about others. With a healthy foundation of self-awareness, resiliency can develop and grow.

TEACHING POINTS

★ Recognizing and respecting uniqueness develops our ability to interact harmoniously in our classroom, school, family, neighborhood and community.

★ Persons of different skin color, height, size, and ability or disability are unique in their own individual ways.

★ We also share similarities with others.

★ We are better able to befriend others and bond socially when we understand and appreciate their lives.

★ Differences enrich our lives, adding diversity and variety.

MATERIALS

★ *People* by Peter Spier. Doubleday Book, 1980

LEARNING ACTIVITY: *People*

1. Read from *People*.

2. Discuss the ways that people are similar and unique. Include appearance, clothing, languages, food, customs and celebrations.

DISCUSSION

1. Give examples from your own neighborhood and friendships of how people are unique yet similar.

2. Talk about someone who is different from you and who is your friend.

RESILIENCY 1: SELF-AWARENESS SKILLS (K-2)

MY FAMILY IS SPECIAL

MAIN IDEA

Self-awareness is recognizing and appreciating how each of us is unique and special. This includes our personal qualities and skills, and the ways in which we grow, learn and thrive. At the same time, we learn to appreciate and respect what is distinct and similar about others. With a healthy foundation of self-awareness, resiliency can develop and grow.

TEACHING POINTS

★ Recognizing and respecting differences among families develops our ability to interact harmoniously in our classroom, school, family, neighborhood and community.

★ Persons with different families share similarities, yet also have their own unique qualities that makes them special.

★ We also share similarities with others.

★ We are better able to befriend others and bond socially when we understand and appreciate their lives.

★ Differences enrich our lives, adding diversity and variety.

MATERIALS

★ *My Family Is Special* activity sheet

LEARNING ACTIVITY: *My Family Is Special*

1. Use examples of how families are unique yet similar: some families have one parent at home; some families have children who live part of the time with one parent and part of the time with another; some children live in foster care. Ask for more examples including; some children who live with two parents of the same gender. Be sure to include a cross-section of family structures and dynamics.

2. Celebrate the uniqueness of families by having each child complete the *My Family Is Special* activity sheet and share it with others. Support everyone's unique family.

DISCUSSION

1. What did you learn about the families of other kids?

2. What is something you enjoyed hearing about someone else's family life that you would enjoy having in your family?

Name_____ Date_____

RESILIENCY 1: Self-Awareness Skills (K-2)
MY FAMILY IS SPECIAL

DRAW OR PASTE A PICTURE OF YOU WITH YOUR FAMILY.

WHAT IS SPECIAL ABOUT YOUR FAMILY?

_____

_____

_____

_____

_____

_____

RESILIENCY 2: EMOTIONAL SKILLS (K-2)

WHAT'S THE FEELING?

MAIN IDEA

Expression of emotions, especially positive emotions, using a vocabulary of "feeling words" builds resiliency. Positive emotions influence a resilient response to adversity.

TEACHING POINTS

★ Our emotions—feelings—are what make us human. Feelings are neither right nor wrong. Feelings are personal, yet everyone experiences similar kinds of feelings.

★ When we identify and express our feelings appropriately, we are better able to communicate with others.

★ We are so wonderfully alive and responsive to what's going on in our lives that we can have several different feelings in a day.

MATERIALS

★ *Feeling Faces* activity sheet

LEARNING ACTIVITY: *What's the Feeling?*

1. Have the children pair up. Hand out the *Feeling Faces* activity sheet; review the feelings.

2. Read a sentence and ask the children to decide which face describes the feeling that matches the sentence. For example:
   "When I see other kids having fun in a playground, I feel_____."
   "When I go to school, I feel_____."
   "I feel_____when my friends refuse to play with me."

3. Add more sentences.

DISCUSSION

1. Which of the feelings on the *Feeling Faces* activity sheet have you felt?

2. Why is it important to put words to our feelings?

RESILIENCY 2: Emotional Skills (K-2)
Feeling Faces

RESILIENCY 2: EMOTIONAL SKILLS (K-2)
BOX OF FEELINGS

MAIN IDEA

Expression of emotions, especially positive emotions, using a vocabulary of "feeling words" builds resiliency. Positive emotions influence a resilient response to adversity.

TEACHING POINTS

★ Our emotions—feelings—are what make us human. Feelings are neither right nor wrong. Feelings are personal, yet everyone experiences similar kinds of feelings.

★ When we identify and express our feelings appropriately, we are better able to communicate with others.

★ We are so wonderfully alive and responsive to what's going on in our lives that we can have several different feelings in a day.

MATERIALS

★ *Box of Feelings* cut into strips, put into a box.

LEARNING ACTIVITY: *Box of Feelings*

1. Tell the children that you've brought a box of feelings with you today. Have the children choose a feeling strip from the box and make up a sentence with the feeling in it. For example, "I felt very sad when our family dog died."

2. Next, tell them about a situation, and ask for a feeling response. For example, "I have an important announcement: our field trip to the petting zoo has been cancelled." Or "because of the heavy rain, recess is cancelled."

DISCUSSION

1. Which of the feelings in the box have you felt before?

2. Why is it important to express our feelings in words?

3. Can kids have different feelings about the same situation?

Box Of Feelings

Directions: Cut up word strips and place in box labeled "Box Of Feelings."

HAPPY	**SAD**
LONELY	**DISAPPOINTED**
ANGRY	**ASHAMED**
SCARED	**SILLY**
SURPRISED	**CONFUSED**
LOVING	**MEAN**
PROUD	**JOYFUL**
EXCITED	**GRUMPY**
BRAVE	**GLAD**
CHEERFUL	**SHOCKED**
NASTY	**ANNOYED**
NERVOUS	**HOPEFUL**
WORRIED	**SORRY**
CALM	**SAFE**

RESILIENCY 2: EMOTIONAL SKILLS (K-2)
FEELING FACE MASKS

MAIN IDEA

Expression of emotions, especially positive emotions, using a vocabulary of "feeling words" builds resiliency. Positive emotions influence a resilient response to adversity.

TEACHING POINTS

★ Our emotions—feelings—are what make us human. Feelings are neither right nor wrong. Feelings are personal, yet everyone experiences similar kinds of feelings.

★ When we identify and express our feeling appropriately, we are better able to communicate with others.

★ We are so wonderfully alive and responsive to what's going on in our lives that we can have several different feelings in a day.

MATERIALS

★ two paper plates per child

★ crayons and markers

★ tongue depressors

★ glue and other materials for decorating the paper plate masks

LEARNING ACTIVITY: *Feeling Face Masks*

1. Tell the children to use one paper plate to create a feeling face mask that shows an emotion that they have recently exprienced. Attach a tongue depressor as a handle for the feeling face mask.

2. Tell the children to create a second paper plate face mask that shows a different emotion.

3. Now, have them write a sentence using the feeling word that describes each face: "I felt sad when my dog died" or "I was very happy when my soccer team won the championship game." Ask the children to show their feeling face masks and read their sentences.

DISCUSSION

1. How do you feel showing your face mask and sharing your feeling sentence?

2. What do you feel when you listen to others share their feelings?

ANGRY ANIMAL

MAIN IDEA

Expression of emotions, especially positive emotions, using a vocabulary of "feeling words" builds resiliency. Positive emotions influence a resilient response to adversity.

TEACHING POINTS

★ We are responsible for the actions that come from our feelings. We can strengthen our ability to manage feelings we don't like having.

★ When we express our feelings we communicate better with people.

★ When we are sad, lonely, scared or angry, we can tell someone we trust such as our parents, family member or teacher.

★ We can also ask this trusted person to help us.

MATERIALS

★ chalkboard, whiteboard or chart paper

★ *Angry Animal* activity sheet

LEARNING ACTIVITY: *Angry Animal*

1. Direct the children to recall a time when they felt angry. What did they do? Write down their different responses (screamed, threw a rock, cried, etc.) on the board.

2. Write one of the angry responses on the board and ask the children how the anger situation was solved.

3. Now ask them how the anger situation could have been managed better. For example, what would have been a non-violent, peaceful and cooperative way to handle the situation? Write these responses on the board, being sure to validate the children's different ways of managing their angry feelings.

4. Hand out the *Angry Animal* activity sheet. Read the beginning of the story. Then invite the children to choose animal names for themselves and finish the story by describing how the animal deals effectively with its anger.

5. Conclude the activity by having them share their stories.

DISCUSSION

1. What did you learn about managing angry feelings?

2. Why is it important to learn ways to manage your angry feelings?

3. Have you ever gone to a trusted person to share a feeling? Were you helped?

Name_____ Date_____

ANGRY ANIMAL
By

_____

(Name your Angry Animal)

Today, we were lining up to go to lunch and I felt so happy that I was first in line.

Suddenly, Larry Lizard jumped right in front of me. I felt angry and...

_____

_____

_____

_____

_____

_____

_____

_____

_____

RESILIENCY 2: EMOTIONAL SKILLS (K-2)

HOW WOULD YOU FEEL IF... WHAT WOULD YOU DO?

MAIN IDEA

Expression of emotions, especially positive emotions, using a vocabulary of "feeling words" builds resiliency. Positive emotions influence a resilient response to adversity.

TEACHING POINTS

★ We are responsible for the actions that come from our feelings. They affect other people—either positively or negatively. We can strengthen our ability to express our feelings appropriately.

★ "Appropriately" means we ask ourselves, "Would I want to be treated this way?" or "How would I feel being treated this way?"

MATERIALS

★ *How Would You Feel If... What Would You Do?* activity sheet

LEARNING ACTIVITY: *How Would You Feel If... What Would You Do?*

1. Tell the children they are going to play a game called *How Would You Feel If... and What Would You Do?* Read each *How Would You Feel If...?* situation from the activity sheet.

2. Invite the children to identify the feeling related to that situation and then write in *What Would You Do?*

3. Complete the list. Elicit responses that are self-empowering, assertive and respectful of the feelings of others.

DISCUSSION

1. What is something you learned about expressing a feeling?

2. Is there more than one way to express a feeling? Why?

3. What's the likely result of showing anger toward another person?

4. Why is it better to express feelings with respect for someone else? What is likely to happen when we do?

Name _____

Date _____

RESILIENCY 2: EMOTIONAL SKILLS (K-2)

HOW WOULD YOU FEEL IF... WHAT WOULD YOU DO?

HOW WOULD YOU FEEL IF...	FEELING	WHAT WOULD YOU DO?
your friend accidentally spills water on you?		
a classmate takes something of yours without asking?		
another kid breaks your favorite toy?		
a kid in the schoolyard calls you a nasty name?		
some friends don't include you in their game?		
some kids laugh at your mistake?		
someone hides your lunch and you can't find it?		
a friend is sad because his dog died?		
a friend sleeping over at your home is scared and wants to go home?		
a bully cuts in front of you in line?		
your friend is crying because she got hurt on the playground?		
a new child feels lonely because no one plays with him at recess?		

CALLING 9-1-1

MAIN IDEA

Communication skills are essential in everyday life. Communication is how we give or receive information. Communication can be verbal or non-verbal. Strengthening communication skills builds resiliency for coping with many different situations.

TEACHING POINTS

★ There are many reasons why we communicate: sometimes to connect with our friends; sometimes to give information; sometimes to ask for help from adults for others or ourselves.

★ Sometimes communicating means asking for help in situations that involve health and safety.

MATERIALS

★ *Calling 9-1-1* handout for parents

LEARNING ACTIVITY: *Calling 9-1-1*

1. Today, we're going to learn how we communicate on the telephone by dialing 9-1-1 to ask special workers to send help in an emergency.

2. You call 9-1-1 in an emergency when an adult is not present. What is an emergency? A fire in your house; someone is unconscious; someone is trying to break into your home.

3. Teach the children what is not an emergency. Examples: lost pet, skinned knee and stolen bicycle. Teach that if the child is in doubt, he should call 9-1-1—better to be safe than sorry. Don't ever call 9-1-1 as a joke.

4. What do you say to 9-1-1? Say, "I need help." Then listen carefully for their questions. What is your address? Where do you live? What is your emergency? What is the problem? Who needs help? Is the person awake and breathing? Is the person bleeding? It's okay to trust the 9-1-1 operator and give him/her your information.

5. It's okay to be frightened in an emergency, but it's important to stay calm and speak slowly, clearly and loudly.

6. Do not hang up. The operator will stay on the phone with you until help arrives.

7. Have the children role-play calling 9-1-1 with an adult playing the 9-1-1 operator. Instruct them to be supportive of others' efforts.

DISCUSSION

1. Have you or anyone you know ever called 9-1-1? What happened?

2. What is the job of a 9-1-1 operator? What other kinds of emergency workers are found in your community? What do they do?

3. Would you like to be a 9-1-1 emergency worker someday—or another kind of emergency helper in your community? Why?

TEACHING YOUR CHILD HOW TO USE 9-1-1

from the health experts of Nemours

One of the challenges you have as a parent is to help your child acquire the skills to work through whatever obstacles life presents. Teaching your child how to use 911 in an emergency could be one of the simplest - and most important - lessons you'll ever share.

Talking About 9-1-1 With Your Child

Not that many years ago, there was a separate telephone number for each type of emergency agency. For a fire, you called the fire department number. For a crime, you called the police. For a medical situation, you phoned the ambulance or doctor.

In 1968, the U.S. government worked with the phone company to establish 9-1-1 as a central number for all types of emergencies. An emergency dispatch operator quickly takes information from the caller and puts the caller in direct contact with whatever emergency personnel are needed, thus making response time quicker.

According to the National Emergency Number Association, 9-1-1 covers nearly all of the population of the United States. Check your phone book to ensure that 9-1-1 is the emergency number you should use in your area.

Everyone needs to know about calling 9-1-1 in an emergency. But children in particular need specifics about what an emergency is. Asking your child, "What would you do if we had a fire in our house?" or "What would you do if you saw someone trying to break in?" gives you a chance to discuss what constitutes an emergency and what should be done if one occurs. Role playing is an especially good way to address various emergency scenarios and give your child the confidence he or she will need to handle them.

For younger children, it might also help to talk about who the emergency workers are in your community - police officers, firefighters, paramedics, doctors, nurses, and so on - and what kinds of things they do to help people who are in trouble. This will paint a clear picture for your little one of not only what types of emergencies can occur, but also who can help.

When to Call 9-1-1

Learning what is an emergency goes hand in hand with learning what isn't. A fire, an intruder in the home, an unconscious family member - these are all things that would require a call to 9-1-1. A skinned knee, a stolen bicycle, or a lost pet wouldn't. Still, teach your child that if ever in doubt and there's no adult around to ask to always make the call. It's much better to be safe than sorry.

Make sure your child understands that calling 9-1-1 as a joke is a crime in many places. In some cities, officials estimate that as much as 75% of the calls made to 9-1-1 are nonemergency calls. These are not all pranks. Some people accidentally push the emergency button on their cell phones. Others don't realize that 9-1-1 is for true emergencies only. That means it's not for such things as a flat tire or even about a theft that occurred the week before.

Stress to your child that whenever an unnecessary call is made to 9-1-1, it can delay a response to someone who actually needs it. Most areas now have what is called enhanced 9-1-1, which enables a call to be traced to the location from which it was made. So if someone dials 9-1-1 as a prank, emergency personnel could be dispatched directly to that location. Not only could this mean life or death for someone having a real emergency on the other side of town, it also means that it's very likely the prank caller will be caught and punished.

How to Use 9-1-1

Although most 9-1-1 calls are now traced, it's still important for your child to have your street address and phone number memorized. Your child will need to give that information to the operator as a confirmation so time isn't lost sending emergency workers to the wrong address.

Make sure your child knows that even though he or she shouldn't give personal information to strangers, it's OK to trust the 911 operator. Walk him or her through some of the questions the operator will ask, including:
- Where are you calling from? (Where do you live?)
- What type of emergency is this?
- Who needs help?
- Is the person awake and breathing?

Explain to your child that it's OK to be frightened in an emergency, but that it's important to stay calm, speak slowly and clearly, and give as much detail to the 9-1-1 operator as possible. If your child is old enough to understand, also explain that the emergency dispatcher may give first-aid instructions before emergency workers arrive at the scene.

Make it clear that your child should **not** hang up until the person on the other end says it's OK, otherwise important instructions or information could be missed.

More Safety Tips

Here are some additional safety tips to keep in mind:

- Always refer to the emergency number as "nine-one-one" not "nine-eleven." In an emergency, your child may not know how to dial the number correctly because of trying to find the "eleven" button on the phone.

- Make sure your house number is clearly visible from the street so that police, fire, or ambulance workers can easily locate your address.

- If you live in an apartment building, make sure your child knows the apartment number and floor you live on.

- Keep a list of emergency phone numbers handy near each phone for your children or babysitter. This should include police, fire, and medical numbers (this is particularly important if you live in one of the few areas where 911 is not in effect), as well as a number where you can be reached, such as your cell phone, pager, or work number. In the confusion of an emergency, calling from a printed list is simpler than looking in the phone book or figuring out which is the correct speed-dial number. The list should also include known allergies, especially to any medication, medical conditions, and insurance information.

- If you have special circumstances in your house, such as an elderly grandparent or a person with a heart condition, epilepsy, or diabetes living in your home, prepare your child by discussing specific emergencies that could occur and how to spot them.

- Keep a first-aid kit handy and make sure your child and babysitters know where to find it. When your child is old enough, teach him or her basic first aid.

This information was provided by KidsHealth, one of the largest resources online for medically reviewed health information written for parents, kids, and teens. For more articles like this one, visit KidsHealth.org or TeensHealth.org. © 1995-2008. The Nemours Foundation. All rights reserved.

✂   Cut along the dotted line.   ✂

EMERGENCY INFORMATION CARD

Fill out all the information that applies to your family and post near the telephone.
Teach your child where it is and how to read the information.

My name is _____

My mother's/father's/guardian's (circle one) name is _____

My mother's/father's/guardian's (circle one) name is _____

My street address is _____ Apartment number _____

City _____Zip Code _____

My nearest cross streets are _____

My house phone number is _____

My mother's/father's/guardian's phone number is _____

My family members have the following allergies/medical conditions/medications

_____

ASSERT YOURSELF

MAIN IDEA

Communication skills are essential in everyday life. Communication is how we give or receive information. Communication can be verbal or non-verbal. Strengthening communication skills builds resiliency for coping with many different situations.

TEACHING POINTS

* Sometimes we need to speak up for ourselves. This is called being assertive.
* When we speak assertively, we are being strong and confident.
* Assertive does not mean threatening others or yelling at them.

MATERIALS

* chalkboard, whiteboard or chart paper

LEARNING ACTIVITY: *Assert Yourself*

1. Ask the children to give some examples of situations in which it is appropriate to be assertive (when you're being bossed around, threatened, called mean names or being pressured to do something that you don't want to do). Ask them how they would feel in these situations.

2. Ask the children for suggestions about what they should do if they were being called mean names. List their responses on the board or chart paper.
   • If they say, "Tell an adult," respond that telling the adult is one way to solve the problem, but then ask, "Is there another way?" Ask them how they might deal with the situation themselves.

3. Guide them into an assertive way of responding and give them an example of how to do it when they're being called names.
   • The child tells the name-caller how her behavior makes her feel.
     "I feel angry because you're calling me names."
   • The child tells the name-caller to stop.
     "Stop calling me names."
   • If the name-calling continues, the child should find an adult to help.

4. Now role-play some of the situations from the list of their responses. First, you role-play a child behaving inappropriately and choose a child to practice how to be assertive. Next, ask two other children to role-play a different situation. Continue until everyone has had a turn to practice.

DISCUSSION

1. What did you learn about speaking assertively?

2. In what kind of situations do we use our assertive communication skills?

SPEAKING AND LISTENING COURTESY

MAIN IDEA

Communication skills are essential in everyday life. Communication is how we give or receive information. Communication can be verbal or non-verbal. Strengthening communication skills builds resiliency for coping with many different situations.

TEACHING POINTS

★ Courteous speaking and courteous listening are essential to communication.

★ What does "courteous" mean? It means being polite, caring about and respecting others.

MATERIALS

★ chalkboard, whiteboard or chart paper

LEARNING ACTIVITY: *Speaking And Listening Courtesy*

1. Ask for two volunteers. Tell them to talk about what they did at recess at school.

2. Point out that in verbal communication there is a speaker and a listener. When one person speaks, the other person listens to what is being said. In a "conversation" both people take turns speaking and listening. Tell the children that speaking and listening are communication skills that can be learned. Say, "I am sure that all of you want to be courteous speakers—and courteous listeners. We're going to learn how to do that today."

3. Ask the children to suggest some important "listening courtesy" skills and write their suggestions on the board or chart paper. Include: look at the speaker; don't interrupt; show you are listening by nodding or by making comments such as "that's neat," etc.; allow speaker to finish speaking; ask any questions after the speaker finishes talking.

4. Do the same for "speaking courtesy" skills. Include: think about what you want to say before you speak; look at the listener; speak clearly; speak up so you can be heard; use polite words; stay on your topic.

5. List some topics of conversation on the board (taking care of a pet, favorite game, favorite sport to play and why, favorite family member or relative, favorite food/treat).

6. Instruct the children to divide into pairs: one will be the speaker and the other will be the listener. The speakers will practice speaking courteously on one of the topics on the board while the other listens courteously. Have them role-play a conversation for one-two minutes, then switch roles for another one-two minutes.

DISCUSSION

1. How did you feel being the speaker? How did you feel being the listener?

2. How do "speaking and listening courtesy" skills help you communicate better at school, at home, in your neighborhood?

ASKING FOR HELP

MAIN IDEA

Communication skills are essential in everyday life. Communication is how we give or receive information. Communication can be verbal or non-verbal. Strengthening communication skills builds resiliency for coping with many different situations.

TEACHING POINTS

★ Sometimes we communicate to make our needs known or to ask for help from adults.

MATERIALS

★ chalkboard, whiteboard or chart paper

LEARNING ACTIVITY: *Asking for Help*

1. Tell the children that they are going to learn how to ask for help from adults.

2. Ask them to suggest situations in which they might need to ask for help and list them on the board or chart paper (kids are fighting on the playground; someone's injured; a stranger is bothering you; you're being bullied; a girl fell off the monkey bars and is crying; a sudden nosebleed).

3. Ask the children for words they can use. Get examples: "I need help," or "Please help me" or "A boy is hurt on the playground—he needs help."

4. Tell them they need to speak loudly, clearly and slowly so the adult understands.

5. In an emergency, they may need to interrupt adults who are talking. Assure them it is okay to interrupt when someone needs immediate help. Tell them they can use words such as, "Excuse me—this is important" or "Excuse me—this is an emergency."

6. Ask a child to role-play a situation from the list that is written on the board or chart paper.

7. Now have them pair up; one will play the child and one will play the adult. In front of everybody, each pair role-plays asking for help. Then they switch roles. Instruct the children to be supportive of others.

DISCUSSION

1. How did you feel getting help for someone?

2. Have you ever been in a situation where you needed to ask for help? What was it like? How did you do it?

3. Now that you've been practicing asking for help, how will you do it differently in the future?

RESILIENCY 4: CONFLICT SOLUTION SKILLS (K-2)
RESPECTING DIFFERENCES

MAIN IDEA

Solving problems, conflicts and disagreements with words instead of with physical force promotes self-confidence and develops resiliency.

TEACHING POINTS

★ Differences make us unique—differences in our preferences, ideas and opinions.

★ Sometimes differences become conflicts. What is "conflict"? Invite answers: conflict is when people can't agree; when kids shout and yell at one another.

MATERIALS

★ two puppets (give them names)

LEARNING ACTIVITY: *Respecting Differences*

1. Portray a conflict situation using two puppets. Demonstrate arguing or being mean. Invite children to describe what they see happening. Ask, "If Billy the puppet were a real boy, how would he feel?"

2. Next, portray a different conflict situation that has a positive outcome. Again, invite the children to describe what they see and hear. Ask, "If Billy the puppet were a real boy, how would he feel?"

3. Now ask the children to give examples of a conflict they had and how it ended. Ask, "Did this end fairly or not?" If it ended fairly, what skills were used to make it end that way? If not, what skills could have been used? Encourage participation by inviting the children to suggest some conflict solution skills that are fair to everyone (listen calmly to each other, figure out a solution together, apologize, ask a trusted adult for help, take turns, or flip a coin).

DISCUSSION

1. What did we learn today about how to solve conflicts?

2. Why is it better to settle conflicts fairly?

3. Which new skill would you like to begin using?

4. Do you know someone who is good at solving conflicts? What skill does she use?

RESILIENCY 4: CONFLICT SOLUTION SKILLS (K-2)

IS IT FAIR?

MAIN IDEA

Solving problems, conflicts and disagreements with words instead of with physical force promotes self-confidence and develops resiliency.

TEACHING POINTS

★ Solving conflict peacefully and cooperatively requires listening carefully and speaking clearly, taking turns, cooperating, compromising and sharing.

MATERIALS

★ none

LEARNING ACTIVITY: *Is It Fair?*

1. Use a story to teach conflict solution skills. Stories can introduce or reinforce conflict solution skills, provide non-threatening ways to talk about conflict, and show characters learning to solve conflicts fairly and cooperatively.

2. Read *Is It Fair?* story below:

Harry the Hippo and Zeke the Zebra were playing ball together. Timothy the Tiger came running up and said, " Hey, that's my ball. Give it to me." Harry the Hippo said, "No, we're playing with it, and besides...it's not yours." Timothy the Tiger grabbed the ball from Zeke the Zebra and they both fell to the ground struggling to hold on to the ball.

3. Ask the children how they think Harry the Hippo and Zeke the Zebra feel.

4. Have them identify the conflict between Harry the Hippo and Zeke the Zebra.

5. Brainstorm ways that the characters could peacefully solve the conflict.

DISCUSSION

1. Discuss the ways the characters could solve their conflict. What would be the best solution? Why?

2. How do you suppose Harry the Hippo and Zeke the Zebra will feel after they peacefully solve their conflict?

RESILIENCY 4: CONFLICT SOLUTION SKILLS (K-2)

PEACEFUL AND COOPERATIVE SOLUTIONS

MAIN IDEA

Solving problems, conflicts and disagreements with words instead of with physical force promotes self-confidence and develops resiliency.

TEACHING POINTS

★ Conflict sometimes happens when people can't agree about something.

★ Sometimes during a conflict one person may make the other person feel badly by using hurtful language or shouting.

★ Using words is a positive way to solve conflict.

MATERIALS

★ two puppets

LEARNING ACTIVITY: *Peaceful And Cooperative Solutions*

1. Discuss what the words conflict, disagreement and argument mean. Ask children for examples from their experiences at school, home, neighborhood, etc. What was the conflict about? With whom? How did it end?

2. Using one puppet yourself and one for the child, role-play one of the conflicts. Ask for suggestions for how this conflict can end peacefully and cooperatively.

3. Let the children give as many solutions as possible (listen carefully to what the arguing person is saying; ask the person to say the problem again if you don't understand; stay calm; if there is no solution, walk away; call an adult).

4. Role-play several of the peaceful and cooperative solutions.

5. Summarize three steps to conflict solution:
       LISTEN—carefully to the conflict (disagreement, argument).
       ASK—the arguing person to stop that behavior.
       CALL—an adult if the conflict can't be solved with words.

DISCUSSION

1. What did we learn today about how to solve conflicts?

2. Why is it better to settle conflicts peacefully and cooperatively?

3. How do you feel being part of settling a conflict?

RESILIENCY 4: CONFLICT SOLUTION SKILLS (K-2)

LEARNING A NEW WAY

MAIN IDEA

Solving problems, conflicts and disagreements with words instead of with physical force promotes self-confidence and develops resiliency.

TEACHING POINTS

★ We all respond differently to conflict.
★ When we become aware of how we respond, we have the opportunity to learn a new way.
★ Solving conflict peacefully helps us become more resilient.

MATERIALS

★ conflict pictures (on the following three pages)

LEARNING ACTIVITY: *Learning A New Way*

1. Show the first conflict picture to the children and tell a story of a conflict based on the picture. For example, you might say, "This is Sarah. Look at her face. Let me tell you what happened to her. One day, Sarah asked two friends if she could play with them in the playhouse. Her friends said, 'No, we're busy!' and they whispered something about her to each other. How do you think that made Sarah feel? What do you think Sarah could do?"

2. Review the three steps to conflict solution:
LISTEN—carefully to the conflict (disagreement, argument).
ASK—the arguing person to stop that behavior.
CALL—an adult if the conflict can't be solved with words.

3. She could ask the children to brainstorm what Sarah could try. She could ask the girls again if she could play with them, find someone else to play with, or ask an adult for help..

4. Repeat steps 1-3 for the next two pictures.

DISCUSSION

1. What have we learned about how to solve a conflict?

2. How do you feel knowing you can improve a bad situation?

RESILIENCY 4: CONFLICT SOLUTION SKILLS (K-2)

LEARNING A NEW WAY
WHAT IS THE CONFLICT? HOW COULD YOU SOLVE THE CONFLICT?

RESILIENCY 4: CONFLICT SOLUTION SKILLS (K-2)

LEARNING A NEW WAY

WHAT IS THE CONFLICT? HOW COULD YOU SOLVE THE CONFLICT?

RESILIENCY 4: CONFLICT SOLUTION SKILLS (K-2)

LEARNING A NEW WAY

WHAT IS THE CONFLICT? HOW COULD YOU SOLVE THE CONFLICT?

WHAT IS BULLYING?

MAIN IDEA

Developing assertiveness skills helps us resist bullying and strengthen resiliency. Everyone has the right to be respected and to feel safe—in school, at home and in neighborhoods.

TEACHING POINTS

★ Bullying is threatening, frightening or harming others.

★ Nobody has the right to make you feel bad or to hurt you.

★ You don't have to accept being bullied. Adults can help.

MATERIALS

★ none

LEARNING ACTIVITY: *What Is Bullying?*

1. Facilitate a discussion about bullying. What is bullying? It could be hitting, punching, pushing or shoving a kid out of line, demanding money, taunting, name-calling, racial slur, ganging-up on a kid, spreading nasty lies about a person, making harassing phone calls, sending text messages or excluding a kid from a group.

2. What's the difference between playful teasing and hurtful bullying? Discuss the difference between harmless fun and mean-spirited, hurtful taunting.

3. We learned that we are all unique. We all have the right to be who we are—we look different, have different abilities, different size families, and different social, cultural and religious customs. No one should be bullied for being different.

What can you do about bullying?
- Tell a trusted adult (teacher, parents, principal, coach). Adults care and want to help.
- Avoid fighting. Violence doesn't solve the problem; it makes it worse.
4. - Tell the bully in a strong, confident way, "Stop doing that." First, practice this.
- Try to be with friends on the bus, in the cafeteria, between classes, or while walking to and from school.
- Choose friends who are supportive and who will include you in their activities.

DISCUSSION

1. How does knowing what to do about bullying help you feel safe?

2. What did you learn today about resisting being bullied?

CALL ME BY MY NAME

MAIN IDEA

Developing assertiveness skills helps us resist bullying and strengthen resiliency. Everyone has the right to be respected and to feel safe—in school, at home and in neighborhoods.

TEACHING POINTS

* Every child has a name.
* Each child likes to be called by her name or a special nickname.
* Name-calling is bullying; it is hurtful and makes children feel unsafe.
* It's important to speak up if you're being bullied.

MATERIALS

* white construction paper
* crayons and markers

LEARNING ACTIVITY: *Call Me By My Name*

1. Facilitate a discussion about children's names and that everybody should be called by his own name. Ask the children to talk about their names. For example: Do they know what their names mean? Are they named after a person, a special place, a flower? Do they have a nickname?

2. Discuss name-calling. Name-calling can happen when girls or boys look different or there is something different about them (overweight, wearing eyeglasses, non-English speaker). Name-calling is verbal bullying ("Hey, Fatso!" "Geek!" "Weirdo!" "Retard!").

3. Have you been called a bad name? What did you do in that situation? How did you feel? What's something better to say or do? For example: "I don't like that—stop it!" You could tell an adult, walk away or find a friend.

4. Instruct the children to use the construction paper to print their names or nicknames and decorate the paper, filling up the entire space. Encourage them to make it look as beautiful as they feel about their names.

DISCUSSION

1. What makes your name special?

2. How did you feel when you were called a bad name?

3. What can you do when someone calls you a bad name?

RESILIENCY 5: ANTI-BULLYING SKILLS (K-2)

RESISTING BULLYING

MAIN IDEA

Developing assertiveness skills helps us resist bullying and strengthen resiliency. Everyone has the right to be respected and to feel safe—in school, at home and in neighborhoods.

TEACHING POINTS

★ Bullying is threatening, frightening or harming others.
★ Nobody has the right to make you feel bad or hurt you.
★ You don't have to accept being bullied. Adults can help.

MATERIALS

★ none

LEARNING ACTIVITY: Resisting Bullying

1. Read one statement at a time or make up your own and then ask, "What can the bullied child do to resist the bully?"

The Statements:
- "When I wake up in the morning, I feel like I don't want to go to school because I'm afraid I'm going to get picked on."
- "In the school yard there are two boys who always laugh at me because I don't talk good English. And then I feel so upset I can't concentrate all day."
- "There's this boy Kevin and he always makes fun of me just because I wear glasses."
- "This kid always pushes me down in the bathroom."
- "These three girls make fun of my clothes."

DISCUSSION

1. How do you feel now that you've learned what to do about being bullied?

2. What have we learned about resisting bullying?

RESILIENCY 5: ANTI-BULLYING SKILLS (K-2)
RESPONSIBILITY

MAIN IDEA

Developing assertiveness skills helps us resist bullying and strengthen resiliency. Everyone has the right to be respected and to feel safe—in school, at home and in neighborhoods.

TEACHING POINTS

★ Bullying violates our right to be who we are. It's when someone threatens, hurts or frightens us.

★ We have a responsibility to protect our friends and others from bullying.

MATERIALS

★ two puppets (give them names)
★ chalkboard, whiteboard or chart paper

LEARNING ACTIVITY: *Responsibility*

1. Introduce the two puppets: one will be a bully and the other will be your friend. Tell them you are going to demonstrate a bullying situation, and afterwards the group will discuss how to deal with this kind of situation.

2. Portray the bullying situation with pushing, name-calling, shoving, etc. Ask the children, "How does it feel to see your friend being bullied? What do you feel like doing about it?" Guide the discussion toward appropriate responses: tell a trusted adult; stand up to the bully yourself; take your friend and walk away together. Encourage more ideas.

DISCUSSION

1. What did you learn today about being a responsible friend?

2. Have you had an experience with a bully? What did you do?

3. What could you now do?

RESILIENCY 6: FRIENDSHIP SKILLS (K-2)
WHAT'S IN MY BAG?

MAIN IDEA

Maintaining closeness, connection and support through friendships are integral components for developing resiliency. Sharing becomes a pathway to building friendships.

TEACHING POINTS

★ Sharing is foundational for building friendships.

MATERIALS

★ Children bring a bag with any five personal objects that are important to them (photo, award, favorite book or toy).

LEARNING ACTIVITY: *What's In My Bag?*

1. Introduce the idea of learning about each other and how sharing personal information helps build friendships.

2. Give the children time to present the objects they brought in and to explain why the objects are important to them.

3. Encourage other children to ask questions.

DISCUSSION

1. How does sharing help us to feel friendly?

2. How does knowing about someone personally build friendships?

RESILIENCY 6: FRIENDSHIP SKILLS (K-2)
FRIENDSHIP PICTURES

MAIN IDEA

Maintaining closeness, connection and support through friendships are integral components for developing resiliency. Sharing becomes a pathway to building friendships.

TEACHING POINTS

★ Sharing is foundational for building friendships.

★ We can look at pictures of friendship to learn about friendship behaviors.

MATERIALS

★ children's photographs, drawings, pictures from the Internet or magazine clippings

LEARNING ACTIVITY: *Friendship Pictures*

1. Ask the children to bring in a picture that shows friendship.

2. Facilitate a discussion. What is friendship: when you and another person like being with each other, playing together, enjoy talking together, and when you have good feelings about another person.

3. Ask each of the children to hold up his friendship picture and tell about it.

DISCUSSION

1. What have we learned today about friendship?

2. How do we build friendships?

RESILIENCY 6: FRIENDSHIP SKILLS (K-2)

STORY TIME

MAIN IDEA

Maintaining closeness, connection and support through friendships are integral components for developing resiliency. Sharing becomes a pathway to building friendships.

TEACHING POINTS

★ Sharing is foundational for building friendships.

★ Reading stories about friends and friendships helps children learn about the special ways in which friendships are formed and maintained.

MATERIALS

★ storybooks

LEARNING ACTIVITY: Story Time

1. Read a story and then ask questions to facilitate a discussion. How are the characters in the story becoming friends? How do they settle their differences or problems?

RECOMMENDED BOOKS:
• A Rainbow of Friends by P.K. Hallinan (Nashville, TN: Ideals Publications, 2001).
• Being Friends by Karen Beaumont (New York: Penguin Putnam Books for Young Readers, 2002).
• Best Friends by Marcia Leonard (Brookfield, CT: Millbrook Press, 1999).
• Chicken Chickens by Valeri Gorbachev (New York: North-South Books, 2001).
• Clifford Makes a Friend by Norman Bridwell (New York: Scholastic, 1998).
• Duck on a Bike by David Shannon (New York: Scholastic, 2002).
• Flip & Flop by Dawn Apperley (New York: Scholastic, 2001).
• Make New Friends by Rosemary Wells (New York: Hyperion, 2002).
• Making Friends by Fred Rogers (New York: Putnam Publishing Group, 1996).
• My Best Friend Moved Away by Nancy L. Carlson (New York: Penguin Putnam Books for Young Readers, 2001).
• My Friend Bear by Jez Alborough (Cambridge, MA: Candlewick Press, 2001).
• The Best of Friends by Pirkko Vainio (New York: North-South Books, 2000).
• The Other Side by Jacqueline Woodson (New York: Penguin USA, 2001).
• The Rainbow Fish by Marcus Pfister (New York, NY: North-South Books, 2000).
• Wemberly Worried by Kevin Henkes (New York: Greenwillow Books, 2000).
• What Will I Do Without You? by Sally Grindley (New York: Scholastic, 1999).
• Where is My Friend? by Marcus Pfister (New York: North-South Books, 2001).
• Will You Be My Friend? by Nancy Tafuri (New York: Scholastic, 2000).
• Will You Forgive Me? by Sally Grindley (New York: Kingfisher, 2001).
• Witzy's Best Friends by Suzy Spafford (New York: Scholastic, 2002).

DISCUSSION

1. Say something that you learned about friendship.

2. Why is it important to have friends?

RESILIENCY 6: FRIENDSHIP SKILLS (K-2)
STOP THE MUSIC!

MAIN IDEA

Maintaining closeness, connection and support through friendships are integral components for developing resiliency. Sharing becomes a pathway to building friendships.

TEACHING POINTS

★ Sharing is foundational for building friendships.

MATERIALS

★ MP3/CD player with music

★ chalkboard, whiteboard or chart paper

LEARNING ACTIVITY: *Stop The Music!*

1. To initiate the friend-making process, play some lively music and encourage the children to move, skip, etc.

2. Stop the music and call out something that they will have in common: everyone with brown hair…all children with blue eyes…everyone who is left handed…just boys…everybody whose birthday is in September, October and November, etc.

3. Have the children with that characteristic raise their hands, and form a group. Write on the board the characteristic and the number of children in that group. Resume the music, then stop it, call out a new characteristic and the children do the same as before.

4. After several rounds, have a discussion about what similarities the children have discovered about one another (large families, birthday in the winter months, blonde hair).

DISCUSSION

1. In how many ways are you like other children?

2. How does this help you make friends?

GRADES 3-4 (AGES 8-9) LESSONS

RESILIENCY 1: SELF-AWARENESS SKILLS (3-4)
ALL ABOUT ME

MAIN IDEA

Self-awareness is recognizing and appreciating how each of us is unique and special. This includes our personal qualities and skills, and the ways in which we grow, learn and thrive. At the same time, we learn to appreciate and respect what is distinct and similar about others. With a healthy foundation of self-awareness, resiliency can develop and grow.

TEACHING POINTS

* Each person has a unique pattern of growth and development.
* Dreams, hopes and ambitions are healthy and appropriate as you grow and develop.
* We share similarities with others; we can learn how to appreciate that each of us is unique yet similar.

MATERIALS

* *All About Me* poster sample layout sheet
* large blank poster paper
* pictures from magazines or the Internet
* scissors, glue sticks, crayons and markers
* a current photo of each child

LEARNING ACTIVITY: *All About Me*

1. Use the *All About Me* sample layout sheet as a template for the children's posters. Explain the activity.

2. Instruct the children to cut out pictures that are appropriate for their posters and write in the answers that are requested on the sample sheet.

3. Afterwards, call upon each child to give an *All About Me* presentation. Display the completed posters.

DISCUSSION

1. What have you learned about yourself from making this poster?

2. What have you learned about someone else that surprised you?

3. What do the posters have in common? How are they different?

Name_____   Date_____

RESILIENCY 1: SELF-AWARENESS SKILLS (3-4)

ALL ABOUT ME

DIRECTIONS: Create a poster that tells others about you. Use photos, pictures from magazines and your own drawings to go with the sentences you write.

MY NAME IS _____ .

I AM _____ **YEARS OLD.**

I AM _____ **FEET TALL.**

MY HAIR COLOR IS _____ .

MY EYES ARE _____ .

PICTURES OF ME
(draw or paste pictures)

FAVORITE COLOR

SOME OF MY FAVORITE THINGS ARE..
(paste in pictures)

SOME THINGS I DO NOT LIKE..
(paste in pictures)

MY PERSONALITY AND CHARACTER
(write about yourself)

I WISH...

MY DREAM IS...

RESILIENCY 1: SELF-AWARENESS SKILLS (3-4)

I AM SPECIAL

MAIN IDEA

Self-awareness is recognizing and appreciating how each of us is unique and special. This includes our personal qualities and skills, and the ways in which we grow, learn and thrive. At the same time, we learn to appreciate and respect what is distinct and similar about others. With a healthy foundation of self-awareness, resiliency can develop and grow.

TEACHING POINTS

★ Each person has special traits and special abilities.

★ We grow and develop emotionally, physically, mentally and socially.

★ We share similarities with others; we can learn how to appreciate that each of us is unique yet similar.

MATERIALS

★ *I Am Special* activity sheet
★ green and blue markers for each child

LEARNING ACTIVITY: *I Am Special*

1. Tell the children that we're going to focus on what makes each of us special and unique. Discuss that all people have unique traits and abilities.

2. Hand out the *I Am Special* activity sheet and markers and instruct the children to follow the directions.

DISCUSSION

1. What have you learned about yourself from doing this activity?

2. Why is it important to recognize what makes us special and unique?

3. What did you learn about someone else?

Name_____ Date_____

I AM SPECIAL

Circle the words that describe special traits about you in GREEN.
Circle the words that describe your special abilities in BLUE.

arts and crafts	drawing	dimples
swimming	brown eyes	wear glasses
creative writing	red hair	girl
science	building things	brown hair
curly hair	math	freckles
boy	computer games	painting
playing sports	green eyes	acting
black hair	inventing	straight hair
blue eyes	reading	blonde hair
baking	listening	skate boarding
speaking more than one language	playing a musical instrument	hazel eyes
helping at home	gymnastics	making friends

RESILIENCY 1: SELF-AWARENESS SKILLS (3-4)

I CAN DO THIS!

MAIN IDEA

Self-awareness is recognizing and appreciating how each of us is unique and special. This includes our personal qualities and skills, and the ways in which we grow, learn and thrive. At the same time, we learn to appreciate and respect what is distinct and similar about others. With a healthy foundation of self-awareness, resiliency can develop and grow.

TEACHING POINTS

★ Each of us has many strengths, and there are also things we want to learn to do better.

★ We can learn to appreciate how each of us wants to do our very best.

MATERIALS

★ *I Can Do This!* activity sheet

★ chalkboard, whiteboard or chart paper

LEARNING ACTIVITY: *I Can Do This!*

1. Hand out the activity sheets, *I Can Do This!* Ask the children to share what they would like to learn to do better. On the board write their names and what they want to do better.

2. Then look at the first child's name and, for example, say: "Stacey, you said you want to learn to be better at spelling." Ask the children to brainstorm how to help Stacey learn to get better at what she wants to do. Have Stacey write down the suggestions on her activity sheet. Then go to the next child and do the same until everyone has had a turn.

3. Now lead the children in an exercise similar to what athletes do to prepare for their own skillful accomplishments: "Relax in your seat...close your eyes...take a deep breath...and let it out. Now picture yourself using the suggestions you wrote down...then say to yourself the words that match what you pictured. For example: I'm feeling great making a speech in front of my class. I can do this! Or I'm running fast and easily winning this race. I can do this!"

DISCUSSION

1. What is it like to see yourself learning to do something better?

2. What is it like for you to help other people learn to do their best?

3. What is it like for you to have others help you to learn to do your best?

Name_____ Date_____

I CAN DO THIS!

_____

Step 1: _____

_____

_____

_____

Step 2: _____

_____

_____

_____

Step 3: _____

_____

_____

_____

Step 4: _____

_____

_____

_____

RESILIENCY I: SELF-AWARENESS SKILLS (3-4)

ONLY ONE OF YOU

MAIN IDEA

Self-awareness is recognizing and appreciating how each of us is unique and special. This includes our personal qualities and skills, and the ways in which we grow, learn and thrive. At the same time, we learn to appreciate and respect what is distinct and similar about others. With a healthy foundation of self-awareness, resiliency can develop and grow.

TEACHING POINTS

★ Each person is unique.

★ We grow and develop emotionally, physically, mentally and socially.

★ We share similarities with others; we can learn how to appreciate how each of us is unique yet similar.

MATERIALS

★ *Only One of You* activity sheet

★ markers, crayons and pencils

LEARNING ACTIVITY: *Only One Of You*

1. Hand out copies of the poem and read it with the children. Have them discuss the messages of the poem.

2. Hand out drawing materials. Ask the children to draw pictures on the activity sheet alongside the poem. Use the children's pictures to facilitate conversations about uniqueness.

DISCUSSION

1. What have we learned from the poem about being unique?

2. Name some ways that people can be different from one another.

3. What would it be like if we were all the same and not all different?

4. Are there some people who look nearly identical to each other? Why? Are they still unique?

Name_____ Date_____

RESILIENCY 1: Self-Awareness Skills (3-4)

ONLY ONE OF YOU

Each of us is different
No one is the same
We all have different faces
Different bodies, different names

Some of us have straight hair
Some of us have curls
Some of us are boys
And some of us are girls

Some of us are tall
Reaching to the sky
While others are quite small
And need help to grab up high

Some of us have blue eyes
And others green or brown
Some can balance on our hands
While standing upside down

Some people like to dance
While others like to sing
And some love to climb trees
So from the branches they can swing

People are like snowflakes
Each one is unique
There are even different moods
For each of the days of the week

All of us are different
It's what makes the world go round
Different smells, different tastes,
Different sights and different sounds

No one is the same
That we know is true
And since each of us is special
There is only one of you.

Jessica Schulder-Orbach

RESILIENCY 1: SELF-AWARENESS SKILLS (3-4)

ACCENTUATE THE POSITIVE

MAIN IDEA

Self-awareness is recognizing and appreciating how each of us is unique and special. This includes our personal qualities and skills, and the ways in which we grow, learn and thrive. At the same time, we learn to appreciate and respect what is distinct and similar about others. With a healthy foundation of self-awareness, resiliency can develop and grow.

TEACHING POINTS

★ Each person has special strengths and special abilities.

★ We share similarities with others; we can learn how to appreciate that each of us is unique yet similar.

MATERIALS

★ none

LEARNING ACTIVITY: *Accentuate The Positive*

1. Divide into groups of four. Have each group focus on one child at a time. Instruct the children to acknowledge the strengths and abilities of that one child. Help them to phrase their acknowledgments using sentence starters such as, "I notice that you…." and "I appreciate the way you…."

2. One child in each group records at least three comments on a sheet of paper and gives it to the child being acknowledged. Continue until all four children have had their turns.

DISCUSSION

1. How do you feel hearing positive statements made about you?

2. Did you learn something about yourself listening to others?

3. Did you hear anything about yourself that surprised you? Describe.

4. How do you feel acknowledging someone else?

MY PERSONAL LETTER

MAIN IDEA

Self-awareness is recognizing and appreciating how each of us is unique and special. This includes our personal qualities and skills, and the ways in which we grow, learn and thrive. At the same time, we learn to appreciate and respect what is distinct and similar about others. With a healthy foundation of self-awareness, resiliency can develop and grow.

TEACHING POINTS

★ Each person has many strengths, and there are also things we want to learn to do better.

★ We can learn to appreciate how each of us wants to learn to do our very best.

★ We share similarities with others; we can learn how to appreciate how each of us is unique yet similar.

MATERIALS

★ a current photo of each child

★ *My Personal Letter* and *My Goals for This Year* activity sheets

LEARNING ACTIVITY: *My Personal Letter*

1. Tell the children they are going to write a letter to themselves and then read those letters again later in the year.

2. Give the children the *My Personal Letter* activity sheet and instruct them to write themselves letters. The letters should describe the children's appearances, families, favorite foods and music, who their friends are, their favorite activities, sports and hobbies, pets, dreams or ambitions.

3. Next, give the children the *My Goals for This Year* activity sheet. Instruct them to write down five goals that they would like to accomplish.

4. Have the children seal and address their letters and address them to themselves. Include their photos with the letters. Collect the letters and store them for later.

5. Later in the year, return the letters to the children and facilitate a discussion about personal growth and change (emotional, physical, mental and social). Instruct them to read their letters and notice what changes they have seen in themselves.

DISCUSSION

1. What new interests have you developed?

2. What new friends have you made?

3. What is something new that you have learned?

4. Have you accomplished your goals? Some of your goals? All of your goals? What helped you reach your goals? Who helped you reach your goals?

Name_____ Date_____

MY PERSONAL LETTER

Dear _____,

_____

_____

_____

_____

_____

_____

_____

_____

_____

_____

_____

_____

_____

_____

Name_____ Date_____

MY GOALS FOR THIS YEAR

Goal 1: _____

_____

_____

Goal 2: _____

_____

_____

Goal 3: _____

_____

_____

Goal 4: _____

_____

_____

Goal 5: _____

_____

_____

RESILIENCY 2: EMOTIONAL SKILLS (3-4)
USING FEELING WORDS

MAIN IDEA

Expression of emotions, especially positive emotions, using a vocabulary of "feeling words" builds resiliency. Positive emotions influence a resilient response to adversity.

TEACHING POINTS

★ Our emotions—feelings—are what make us human. Feelings are neither right nor wrong. Feelings are personal, yet everyone experiences similar kinds of feelings.

★ When we identify our own feelings, we are better able to communicate with others.

★ We are so wonderfully alive and responsive to what's going on in our lives that we can have several different feelings in a day.

MATERIALS

★ chalkboard, whiteboard or chart paper

★ *Feeling Words* handout

★ *Using Feeling Words* activity sheet

LEARNING ACTIVITY: *Using Feeling Words*

1. Ask the children to name different feelings that they've experienced (happy, sad, disappointed, angry, thrilled). Write them on the board or chart paper. Be sure their words describe emotions, not physical sensations (feeling hungry, feeling tired).

2. Give the children the *Using Feeling Words* activity sheet. Tell them to choose a word from the *Feeling Words* handout, write it down and use it in a sentence. Repeat, using more words from the list.

DISCUSSION

1. What new feeling words have you learned?

2. How do you feel knowing that others experience the same feelings as you do?

FEELING WORDS

angry	troubled	annoyed	disappointed	cranky
furious	ticked off	upset	hostile	wary
scared	concerned	amused	hurt	thrilled
glad	excited	pleased	content	awful
lonely	put-down	embarrassed	hopeless	helpless
sorrowful	powerless	useless	unworthy	foolish
awkward	silly	humiliated	happy	nervous
puzzled	shocked	relieved	depressed	anxious
timid	ashamed	suspicious	worried	jittery
uneasy	afraid	confused	frustrated	miserable
elated	calm	pleased	sad	jealous
hopeful	surprised	disgusted	guilty	proud

Name_____ Date_____

USING FEELING WORDS

Feeling Word 1: _____

I feel _____ when _____

_____

_____

Feeling Word 2: _____

I feel _____ when _____

_____

_____

Feeling Word 3: _____

I feel _____ when _____

_____

_____

Feeling Word 4: _____

I feel _____ when _____

_____

_____

Feeling Word 5: _____

I feel _____ when _____

_____

_____

RESILIENCY 2: EMOTIONAL SKILLS (3-4)
BODY LANGUAGE

MAIN IDEA

Expression of emotions, especially positive emotions, using a vocabulary of "feeling words" builds resiliency. Positive emotions influence a resilient response to adversity.

TEACHING POINTS

★ When we use words to communicate feelings, we call this verbal communication.

★ We also communicate non-verbally through our gestures, postures and facial expressions. This is called "body language."

★ When we learn to "read" body language, we improve our ability to understand what other people are feeling and to respond appropriately.

MATERIALS

★ none

LEARNING ACTIVITY: *Body Language*

1. Instruct the children to form two lines—A and B. Have line A face line B so that each child is looking at a partner.

2. Call out a word for an emotion and ask the children in line A to make the face and assume the posture or gesture of that emotion. The children in line B are then asked to copy their partners' facial expressions and body postures.

3. Ask questions: "Do some of the faces and bodies look alike? Do some look different? Do some have the same facial expressions but different postures or gestures?"

4. Now instruct the children in line B to show a new emotion and instruct the children in line A to copy it. Use the same questions.

DISCUSSION

1. Discuss how you recognize what someone is feeling by looking at his body language.

2. What did you learn from seeing your own facial expressions, gestures and posture copied?

3. What did you learn about how others see you?

4. Now that you know what you look like communicating _____ (choose an emotion), do you think you'll be better able to recognize when someone else is feeling _____ (the same emotion)?

S-I-T: MY RESPONSE PLAN

MAIN IDEA

Expression of emotions, especially positive emotions, using a vocabulary of "feeling words" builds resiliency. Positive emotions influence a resilient response to adversity.

TEACHING POINTS

★ Our emotions—feelings—are what make us human. Feelings are neither right nor wrong. Feelings are personal, yet everyone experiences similar kinds of feelings.

★ When we can identify and express our feelings appropriately, we are better able to communicate with others.

★ When something upsetting happens you might feel sad, hopeless, afraid, angry, etc.

★ We can learn how to improve an upsetting situation by using a response plan.

MATERIALS

★ S-I-T: My Response Plan activity sheet

LEARNING ACTIVITY: S-I-T: My Response Plan

1. Have the children give examples of upsetting situations. Tell them they do not have to stay stuck in feeling upset. Here's a response plan to feel better. It's called S-I-T. Hand out the activity sheet and read through it with the kids.
- S = Stop. Just stop what I am doing and calm down. How? Take a few deep breaths (and let them out!), or I could slowly count to ten.
- I = Identify. Ask: "What's troubling me? What's the problem?"
- T = Talk. Who can I turn to for help—my mom or dad, a trusted adult, like a teacher or grandma?

2. Now have the children complete the S-I-T: My Response Plan activity sheet.

DISCUSSION

1. What's another way to calm down besides taking relaxing breaths?

2. Who are the trusted people in your life that you can turn to for help?

3. How do we ask for help? Say, "I need help." What's another way?

4. How do you feel knowing that you have a response plan to get out of being stuck in a negative feeling?

5. How can you use the S-I-T Response Plan to help others get out of their negative feelings?

Name_____ Date_____

S-I-T: MY RESPONSE PLAN

S = STOP
Stop what I am doing. Calm down. How?

1._____

2._____

3._____

I = IDENTIFY
What is the problem?

1._____

2._____

3._____

T = TALK
Who are some trusted adults I can talk to?

1._____

2._____

3._____

RESILIENCY 2: EMOTIONAL SKILLS (3-4)

RESPONDING TO FEELINGS

MAIN IDEA

Expression of emotions, especially positive emotions, using a vocabulary of "feeling words" builds resiliency. Positive emotions influence a resilient response to adversity.

TEACHING POINTS

* When we communicate our feelings though words, we call this verbal communication.

* We also communicate non-verbally through our gestures, postures and facial expressions. This is called "body language."

* When we learn to "read" body language, we improve our ability to understand what others are feeling and to respond appropriately.

MATERIALS

* *List of Feeling Words* handout

LEARNING ACTIVITY: *Responding To Feelings*

1. Tell the children they are going to practice responding to other children's feelings.

2. Have the children divide into groups of four. Hand out the *List of Feeling Words* and ask each group to choose two words from the list.

3. Begin by having each group select one of those two words. Say, "Show us what_____ looks like." One child role-plays looking, speaking and behaving the feeling_____ (sad with facial expression and posture).

4. Next, the group discusses and creates a response to that feeling. One of the group members role-plays the response (kindly gesture, reassuring pat on the back, friendly smile, etc.).

5. Now have the pair role-play the feeling and the response together. Repeat steps 3-5 for the second feeling word.

6. Gather the groups together and ask for one pair of children at a time to role-play the feeling word and the response that they worked on in their small groups.

DISCUSSION

1. What did you learn from role-playing feelings and responses?

2. What did you learn from watching the others role-play feelings and responses?

LIST OF FEELING WORDS

angry	troubled	annoyed	disappointed	cranky
furious	ticked off	upset	hostile	wary
scared	concerned	amused	hurt	thrilled
glad	excited	pleased	content	awful
lonely	put-down	embarrassed	hopeless	helpless
sorrowful	powerless	useless	unworthy	foolish
awkward	silly	humiliated	happy	nervous
puzzled	shocked	relieved	depressed	anxious
timid	ashamed	suspicious	worried	jittery
uneasy	afraid	confused	frustrated	miserable
elated	calm	pleased	sad	jealous
hopeful	surprised	disgusted	guilty	proud

RESILIENCY 2: EMOTIONAL SKILLS (3-4)

EMOTIONS THEATER

MAIN IDEA

Expression of emotions, especially positive emotions, using a vocabulary of "feeling words" builds resiliency. Positive emotions influence a resilient response to adversity.

TEACHING POINTS

★ When we communicate our feelings though words, we call this verbal communication.

★ We also communicate non-verbally through our gestures, postures and facial expressions. This is called "body language."

★ When we learn to "read" body language, we improve our ability to understand what others are feeling and to respond appropriately.

MATERIALS

★ *List of Feeling Words* handout

LEARNING ACTIVITY: *Emotions Theater*

1. Hand out the *List of Feeling Words*, ask the children to love it over and find words that they could portray with their facial expressions, gestures and physical posture.

2. Help children be creative: What would _____(sad, happy, etc.) look like? How would you move if you were feeling _____(sad, happy, etc.)? How would your face, body, eyes, arms and legs look if you were feeling _____(sad, happy, etc.)?

3. Instruct the children to pair up. Invite the group to watch as each pair performs their chosen emotions.

DISCUSSION

1. Discuss how did you feel portraying a specific emotion.

2. Did you correctly "read" other children's body language? Why or why not?

3. What did you learn about yourself and others from this activity?

FEELING WORDS

angry	troubled	annoyed	disappointed	cranky
furious	ticked off	upset	hostile	wary
scared	concerned	amused	hurt	thrilled
glad	excited	pleased	content	awful
lonely	put-down	embarrassed	hopeless	helpless
sorrowful	powerless	useless	unworthy	foolish
awkward	silly	humiliated	happy	nervous
puzzled	shocked	relieved	depressed	anxious
timid	ashamed	suspicious	worried	jittery
uneasy	afraid	confused	frustrated	miserable
elated	calm	pleased	sad	jealous
hopeful	surprised	disgusted	guilty	proud

CONVERSATION COURTESY

MAIN IDEA

Communication skills are essential in everyday life. Communication is how we give or receive information. Communication can be verbal or non-verbal. Strengthening communication skills builds resiliency for coping with many different situations.

TEACHING POINTS

★ Courteous speaking and courteous listening are essential to positive, productive communication.

MATERIALS

★ chalkboard, whiteboard or chart paper

LEARNING ACTIVITY: *Conversation Courtesy*

1. Review the basics of a conversation, including why it's important to speak and listen courteously.

2. Ask the children to suggest some important "listening courtesy" skills. Write their suggestions on the board or chart paper. Make sure to include: look directly at the speaker; don't interrupt; show you are listening by nodding or by making comments; allow speaker to finish; ask your questions after the speaker is done.

3. Do the same for "speaking courtesy" skills. Include: think about what you want to say before you speak; look at the listener; speak clearly; speak up so you can be heard; use polite words; stay on topic; use "My point is…."

4. Ask the children to suggest some topics for conversation practice (favorite TV show, favorite game, favorite sport to play and why, favorite food/treat, favorite family activity). List these on the board or chart paper.

5. Divide into pairs: A is the speaker; B, the listener. A's begin the conversation using a topic of their choice. B's join in, first by being courteous listeners and then courteous speakers. Take a couple of minutes and then switch roles.

DISCUSSION

1. Was it easier being the speaker or being the listener? What was the difference?

2. How did you feel being the speaker? How did you feel being the listener?

3. How can "speaking and listening courtesy" skills help you communicate more effectively in a conversation at school, at home, in your neighborhood?

"I" MESSAGES

MAIN IDEA

Communication skills are essential in everyday life. Communication is how we give or receive information. Communication can be verbal or non-verbal. Strengthening communication skills builds resiliency for coping with many different situations.

TEACHING POINTS

★ "I" messages let others know our feelings without blaming or being mean.
★ "I" messages help us to be assertive—it's how we stand up for ourselves.
★ The "I" message is a strong, clear, confident statement about our needs, ideas and feelings.
★ We use "I" messages to communicate in an appropriate way when we feel upset.
★ When we first learn how to use the "I" message, it may feel unfamiliar. After practicing, you'll feel comfortable expressing yourself in this direct way.

MATERIALS

★ chalkboard, whiteboard or chart paper
★ hat or box
★ "I" Messages cut up into slips of paper

LEARNING ACTIVITY: "I" Messages

1. Here's how to use the "I" message. Write on the board or chart paper: "I feel _____ (say your feeling) when you _____ (describe the person's action) because _____ (say why the action effects you)." Teach the "I" message formula for these situations.
• EXAMPLE: Your friends are talking excitedly and loudly at the lunch table and you want to join in, but they ignore you.
  • "I" message: I feel frustrated when you ignore me because I don't get a chance to say what I'm thinking.
• EXAMPLE: A stronger, bigger kid threatens you if you don't give him a candy bar from your lunch.
  • "I" message: I feel angry when you threaten me because it's unfair to me.

2. Take the hat or box with the folded slips of paper and ask a child to choose one and read it aloud. Have her use an "I" message to respond to the situation.

3. Ask other children to contribute additional "I" messages to that situation.

DISCUSSION

1. How do you feel expressing yourself with an "I" message?

2. Discuss why the "I" message is a good way to express yourself.

RESILIENCY 3: COMMUNICATION SKILLS (3-4)

"I" MESSAGES

Directions: Cut up slips of papers, fold them in half
and put them in a hat or box.

A student in your class makes fun of your drawing.

Your best friend says she doesn't want to be friends with you anymore.

Some friends make fun of what you're wearing.

You make an error in a ball game and some of your teammates ridicule you.

You get blamed for something that is not your fault.

A friend makes fun of your family car.

Your friends exclude you from a playground game.

Your friend asks you to help her steal something from a store.

Your friend returns a board game that he borrowed, but it is missing
some pieces.

You're trying to make friends with a new boy in your neighborhood and
he is unfriendly.

A boy pushes you aside as he runs to play with other kids.

A classmate calls you a mean name because you are overweight.

NON-VERBAL COMMUNICATION

MAIN IDEA

Communication skills are essential in everyday life. Communication is how we give or receive information. Communication can be verbal or non-verbal. Strengthening communication skills builds resiliency for coping with many different situations.

TEACHING POINTS

★ Verbal communication means using our words.

★ Non-verbal communication means using body movements and facial gestures. This is called "body language."

★ Every day we use verbal and non-verbal communication.

★ Our body language "talks." The body language we use sends messages.

★ Both verbal and non-verbal communication reveals our moods, feelings and attitudes.

MATERIALS

★ *Non-Verbal Communication* cut up into slips of paper, put in a box

LEARNING ACTIVITY: *Non-Verbal Communication*

1. Tell the children to think about how we communicate non-verbally. Say, "When I stand here with my arms tightly folded and a scowl on my face, what am I communicating? Is it positive or negative? Now, when you see me smiling and my arms wide open in a gesture of greeting, what am I communicating?"

2. Tell the children that we communicate without speaking. Our body language "talks." Our facial expressions send messages. Non-verbal communication shows our moods, feelings and attitudes. Say, "Watch me. I'm going to let my body 'talk' to you, and you tell me what I'm communicating." One at a time perform various non-verbal communications (tap foot, frown, shake a fist, slouch shoulders and droop head, smile and wave). Discuss what each means.

3. Have each child take a slip of paper from the box and role-play the instructions. Ask the other children to guess what message the facial expression and body movements are communicating. Make sure to ask if the communication is negative or positive.

DISCUSSION

1. How does learning about non-verbal communication help us become better communicators?

2. How does our non-verbal communication affect others?

RESILIENCY 3: COMMUNICATION SKILLS (3-4)

NON-VERBAL COMMUNICATION

Directions: Cut up slips and place in box.

Slouch shoulders and lower head.	Make a snarling, threatening look.
Snap fingers and tap foot.	Stamp foot and shake fist.
Smile and wave arms.	Kick violently.
Look down at floor; let arms hang by side.	Sit in chair with arms and legs crossed tightly.
Crouch in corner with eyes staring down.	Open mouth and fling arms open.
Point finger and scowl.	Smack fist into open palm.
Rub hands together and blow on them.	Rub closed eyes and pout.
Put both hands on hips and stare straight ahead.	Shuffle feet with back hunched forward.
Open palm behind ear with questioning look on face.	Stomp, and shake fists up and down.
Hold stomach and frown.	Face the children with arms out and palms open.
Shake head back and forth and wag finger.	Jump up and down and wave arms and hands in air.
Open arms.	Roll eyes and sigh.

RESPECTFUL STATEMENTS

MAIN IDEA

Communication skills are essential in everyday life. Communication is how we give or receive information. Communication can be verbal or non-verbal. Strengthening communication skills builds resiliency for coping with many different situations.

TEACHING POINTS

★ Words have power: they can be put-downs that disrespect others and hurt their feelings, or they can be words that convey appreciation and respect others.

★ When you use respectful language to communicate with others they are more likely to take you seriously and respond positively to what you are saying.

MATERIALS

★ chalkboard, whiteboard or chart paper

LEARNING ACTIVITY: *Respectful Statements*

1. Facilitate a discussion about respectful and disrespectful language. What do we call words that are insulting and hurtful? Put-downs. How do you feel when you hear a put-down directed at you? How do you feel saying a put-down to someone else? Ask the children to give you examples of put-downs. List the put-down words in a column on the board or chart paper.

2. Now, ask the children for specific words that they use which show respect or appreciation for others. List these in a column next to the put-down column.

3. Which put-downs bother you? Which ones hurt your feelings? Where have you heard put-downs?

4. What respectful statements have you heard in class, in the schoolyard, at home? Have each child say a respectful statement.

DISCUSSION

1. Discuss how others treat you when you speak to them respectfully.

2. Discuss how the world would be better if people stopped using put-downs and spoke to one another using respectful statements.

RESILIENCY 3: COMMUNICATION SKILLS (3-4)

CALLING 9-1-1

MAIN IDEA

Communication skills are essential in everyday life. Communication is how we give or receive information. Communication can be verbal or non-verbal. Strengthening communication skills builds resiliency for coping with many different situations.

TEACHING POINTS

★ There are many reasons why we communicate: sometimes to connect with our friends; sometimes to give information; sometimes to ask for help from adults for others or ourselves.

★ Sometimes, communicating means asking for help in situations that involve health and safety.

MATERIALS

★ chalkboard, whiteboard or chart paper

★ *Teaching Your Child How To Use 9-1-1* handout for parents

LEARNING ACTIVITY: *Calling 9-1-1*

1. Today we are going to review how we communicate on the telephone by dialing 9-1-1 to ask for help in an emergency.

2. Review when to call 9-1-1: in an emergency when an adult is not present. What is an emergency? A fire; someone is seriously hurt or unconscious; someone is trying to break into the home.

3. Review what is not an emergency (lost pet, sprained ankle or stolen bicycle). Teach that if the child is in doubt he/she should call 9-1-1. It is better to be safe than sorry.

4. What do you say to 9-1-1? Say, "I need help." Then listen carefully for their questions. What's your address? Where do you live? What is your emergency? What's the problem? Who needs help? Is the person awake and breathing? Is the person bleeding? It's okay to trust the 9-1-1 operator and give him/her your personal information.

5. It's okay to be frightened in an emergency, but it's also important to stay calm and speak slowly, clearly and loudly.

6. Do not hang up. The operator will stay on the phone with you until help arrives.

7. Have the children role-play calling 9-1-1 with an adult playing the 9-1-1 operator. Instruct them to be supportive of others' efforts.

DISCUSSION

1. Have you or anyone you know ever called 9-1-1? What happened?

2. What is the job of a 9-1-1 operator? What other kinds of emergency workers are found in your community? What do they do?

3. Would you like to be a 9-1-1 emergency worker someday, or another kind of emergency helper in your community? Why?

TEACHING YOUR CHILD HOW TO USE 9-1-1

from the health experts of Nemours

One of the challenges you have as a parent is to help your child acquire the skills to work through whatever obstacles life presents. Teaching your child how to use 911 in an emergency could be one of the simplest - and most important - lessons you'll ever share.

Talking About 9-1-1 With Your Child

Not that many years ago, there was a separate telephone number for each type of emergency agency. For a fire, you called the fire department number. For a crime, you called the police. For a medical situation, you phoned the ambulance or doctor.

In 1968, the U.S. government worked with the phone company to establish 9-1-1 as a central number for all types of emergencies. An emergency dispatch operator quickly takes information from the caller and puts the caller in direct contact with whatever emergency personnel are needed, thus making response time quicker.

According to the National Emergency Number Association, 9-1-1 covers nearly all of the population of the United States. Check your phone book to ensure that 9-1-1 is the emergency number you should use in your area.

Everyone needs to know about calling 9-1-1 in an emergency. But children in particular need specifics about what an emergency is. Asking your child, "What would you do if we had a fire in our house?" or "What would you do if you saw someone trying to break in?" gives you a chance to discuss what constitutes an emergency and what should be done if one occurs. Role playing is an especially good way to address various emergency scenarios and give your child the confidence he or she will need to handle them.

For younger children, it might also help to talk about who the emergency workers are in your community - police officers, firefighters, paramedics, doctors, nurses, and so on - and what kinds of things they do to help people who are in trouble. This will paint a clear picture for your little one of not only what types of emergencies can occur, but also who can help.

When to Call 9-1-1

Learning what is an emergency goes hand in hand with learning what isn't. A fire, an intruder in the home, an unconscious family member - these are all things that would require a call to 9-1-1. A skinned knee, a stolen bicycle, or a lost pet wouldn't. Still, teach your child that if ever in doubt and there's no adult around to ask to always make the call. It's much better to be safe than sorry.

Make sure your child understands that calling 9-1-1 as a joke is a crime in many places. In some cities, officials estimate that as much as 75% of the calls made to 9-1-1 are nonemergency calls. These are not all pranks. Some people accidentally push the emergency button on their cell phones. Others don't realize that 9-1-1 is for true emergencies only. That means it's not for such things as a flat tire or even about a theft that occurred the week before.

Stress to your child that whenever an unnecessary call is made to 9-1-1, it can delay a response to someone who actually needs it. Most areas now have what is called enhanced 9-1-1, which enables a call to be traced to the location from which it was made. So if someone dials 9-1-1 as a prank, emergency personnel could be dispatched directly to that location. Not only could this mean life or death for someone having a real emergency on the other side of town, it also means that it's very likely the prank caller will be caught and punished.

How to Use 9-1-1

Although most 9-1-1 calls are now traced, it's still important for your child to have your street address and phone number memorized. Your child will need to give that information to the operator as a confirmation so time isn't lost sending emergency workers to the wrong address.

Make sure your child knows that even though he or she shouldn't give personal information to strangers, it's OK to trust the 911 operator. Walk him or her through some of the questions the operator will ask, including:
- Where are you calling from? (Where do you live?)
- What type of emergency is this?
- Who needs help?
- Is the person awake and breathing?

RESILIENCY 3: COMMUNICATION SKILLS (3-4)

Explain to your child that it's OK to be frightened in an emergency, but that it's important to stay calm, speak slowly and clearly, and give as much detail to the 9-1-1 operator as possible. If your child is old enough to understand, also explain that the emergency dispatcher may give first-aid instructions before emergency workers arrive at the scene.

Make it clear that your child should **not** hang up until the person on the other end says it's OK, otherwise important instructions or information could be missed.

More Safety Tips

Here are some additional safety tips to keep in mind:

- Always refer to the emergency number as "nine-one-one" not "nine-eleven." In an emergency, your child may not know how to dial the number correctly because of trying to find the "eleven" button on the phone.

- Make sure your house number is clearly visible from the street so that police, fire, or ambulance workers can easily locate your address.

- If you live in an apartment building, make sure your child knows the apartment number and floor you live on.

- Keep a list of emergency phone numbers handy near each phone for your children or babysitter. This should include police, fire, and medical numbers (this is particularly important if you live in one of the few areas where 911 is not in effect), as well as a number where you can be reached, such as your cell phone, pager, or work number. In the confusion of an emergency, calling from a printed list is simpler than looking in the phone book or figuring out which is the correct speed-dial number. The list should also include known allergies, especially to any medication, medical conditions, and insurance information.

- If you have special circumstances in your house, such as an elderly grandparent or a person with a heart condition, epilepsy, or diabetes living in your home, prepare your child by discussing specific emergencies that could occur and how to spot them.

- Keep a first-aid kit handy and make sure your child and babysitters know where to find it. When your child is old enough, teach him or her basic first aid.

This information was provided by KidsHealth, one of the largest resources online for medically reviewed health information written for parents, kids, and teens. For more articles like this one, visit KidsHealth.org or TeensHealth.org. © 1995-2008. The Nemours Foundation. All rights reserved.

✂   Cut along the dotted line.   ✂
- -

EMERGENCY INFORMATION CARD

Fill out all the information that applies to your family and post near the telephone.
Teach your child where it is and how to read the information.

My name is _____

My mother's/father's/guardian's (circle one) name is _____

My mother's/father's/guardian's (circle one) name is _____

My street address is _____ Apartment number _____

City _____Zip Code _____

My nearest cross streets are _____

My house phone number is _____

My mother's/father's/guardian's phone number is _____

My family members have the following allergies/medical conditions/medications

_____

WHAT IS CONFLICT?

MAIN IDEA

Solving problems, conflicts and disagreements with words instead of with physical force promotes self-confidence and develops resiliency.

TEACHING POINTS

★ Conflict can occur when people can't agree about something. Sometimes people argue or use physical force in their conflict.

★ These are some of the essential skills we've learned about solving conflicts peacefully and without hurting one another: listen to each other; together, figure out a solution; show respect for one another; apologize; forgive; take time to cool off; ask an adult for help; know when to walk away.

MATERIALS

★ chalkboard, whiteboard or chart paper

LEARNING ACTIVITY: *What Is Conflict?*

1. Write the word "conflict" on the board and ask the children to brainstorm other words that have similar meanings (disagreement, argument, fight, dispute). Ask the children for examples from their experiences at school, home, neighborhood, etc. What was the conflict about? With whom? How did it end? Write these on the board or chart paper.

2. Select one of the conflicts listed that didn't end well and ask two children to role-play the conflict. Then ask others for suggestions for how this conflict can end peacefully and cooperatively. Discuss the essential skills in the teaching points for solving conflicts.

3. Now ask two other children to role-play one of these peaceful conflict solutions. Ask the role-players how it feels to solve a conflict cooperatively and peacefully. Repeat the process, asking different children to role-play other conflict situations.

DISCUSSION

1. What did we learn today about how to solve conflicts?

2. What are the benefits of settling conflicts peacefully and cooperatively?

3. Now that you are becoming skilled at solving a conflict, what conflicts in the world would you like to settle?

RESILIENCY 4: CONFLICT SOLUTION SKILLS (3-4)

PEACEFUL CONFLICT SOLVING

MAIN IDEA

Solving problems, conflicts and disagreements with words instead of with physical force promotes self-confidence and develops resiliency.

TEACHING POINTS

★ Conflict can occur when people can't agree about something. Sometimes people argue or use physical force in their conflict.

★ These are some of the essential skills we've learned about solving conflicts peacefully and without hurting one another: listen to each other; together, figure out a solution; show respect for one another; apologize; forgive; take time to cool off; ask an adult for help; know when to walk away.

MATERIALS

★ *Peaceful Conflict Solving Cards* cut up and put in a box

LEARNING ACTIVITY: *Peaceful Conflict Solving*

1. Ask the children to share stories about a conflict or argument they had. Tell them that as they talk about the conflict to think about what happened, how it happened and how the conflict ended.

2. Ask one child to pick a *Peaceful Conflict Solving* card and read it. Ask the child how this conflict solving suggestion could have helped. Ask others for their opinions.

3. Choose a second or third card also and repeat the learning activity.

DISCUSSION

1. What is it like to have more than one way to solve a problem or conflict?

2. Why is it better to settle conflicts peacefully?

PEACEFUL CONFLICT SOLVING CARDS

Directions: Cut up cards and use during lesson discussion.

Listen to each other.	Show respect.
Together, figure out a solution.	Forgive one another.
Take time to cool off.	Ask an adult for help.
Know when to walk away.	Apologize.

S-T-O-P:
STOP-THINK-OPTIONS-POSITIVE STEPS

MAIN IDEA

Solving problems, conflicts and disagreements with words instead of with physical force promotes self-confidence and develops resiliency.

TEACHING POINTS

★ We experience emotions all the time. We are so wonderfully alive and responsive to what's going on in our lives that we can have several different feelings in a day.

★ Feelings are what make us uniquely human; they are neither right nor wrong.

★ Sometimes we feel fine and sometimes things happen that make us feel badly. When something upsetting happens you might feel sad, hopeless, angry, etc. You might have negative thoughts, such as "I'm no good."

★ Learning how to recognize and respond appropriately to our upsetting emotions helps develop resiliency.

★ You can learn how to not stay stuck in feeling upset.

MATERIALS

★ S-T-O-P activity sheet

LEARNING ACTIVITY: Stop-Think-Options-Positive Steps

1. You have already learned one tool to successfully confront bad feelings. Review *S-I-T: My Response Plan*.

2. S-T-O-P is another tool.
   • **S = Stop** and calm Down. How? Take some deep, relaxing breaths. What are some other ways I could calm down?
   • **T = Think.** What's troubling me? What's the problem or conflict?
   • **O = Options.** What are my choices? What could I do?
   • **P = Positive Steps.** What steps will I take?

3. Fill out the activity sheets using the S-T-O-P tool. For example, some kids have planned a party and not invited you or a friend tells you she is doing drugs.

DISCUSSION

1. Have you ever felt so upset that you didn't know what to do? What did you do?

2. What are other ways to calm down besides taking relaxing breaths?

3. Who are some trusted, caring people you can talk to?

Name_____ Date_____

S-T-O-P

The situation: _____

_____

_____

S = **STOP.** Calm down. How?

1._____

2._____

3._____

T = **THINK.** What is the problem or conflict?

1._____

2._____

3._____

O = **OPTIONS.** What are my choices? What *could* I do?

1._____

2._____

3._____

P = **POSITIVE STEPS.** What steps *will* I take?

1._____

2._____

3._____

HELPING SOLVE CONFLICTS

MAIN IDEA

Solving problems, conflicts and disagreements with words instead of with physical force promotes self-confidence and develops resiliency.

TEACHING POINTS

★ A conflict is when people can't agree about something. Sometimes people argue or use physical force in their conflict.

★ There are essential skills for solving conflicts peacefully and without hurting one another: listen to each other; together, figure out a solution; show respect for one another; apologize; forgive; take time to cool off; ask an adult for help; know when to walk away.

MATERIALS

★ *Helping Solve Conflicts* prepared scripts

LEARNING ACTIVITY: *Helping Solve Conflicts*

1. Have three children role-play Script 1. After watching the role-play, ask questions to facilitate a discussion.
• What did you see the helper doing?
• Did this kind of "helping" improve the situation?
• What would have worked better?
• What could the helper have done differently?

2. Now, using Script 2, the same role-players demonstrate the skills of how to solve a conflict between people. Ask questions to facilitate a discussion.
• What did you see this time that helped solve the problem?
• What are some actions that the helper did that helped solve the problem?
• How did the people in the conflict respond to the help they received?
• Was their conflict solved?

DISCUSSION

1. How can we have an important role in helping our friends and family solve conflicts?

2. What kind of "helping" does not work?

3. What kind of "helping" really does work?

RESILIENCY 4: CONFLICT SOLUTION SKILLS (3-4)
HELPING SOLVE CONFLICTS

Two boys are arguing about establishing the rules of a ball game they want to play at recess. They can't agree on the basic rules of the game. The arguing gets heated and they start pushing each other and calling one another bad names. The "Helper" steps in.

SCRIPT 1

Helper: Hey...what's going on here? What's the problem?

Billy: He says you're out if the ball goes over the yellow line and I said—

Brandon: No, I didn't, you stupid liar—

Billy: Yes, you did, you jerk.

Helper: That's right, Billy. Stop being a jerk.

Billy: I didn't say that. I said you should be out if the ball touches the yellow line. Touching is out.

Brandon: You don't even know how to play. I've played this game before—

Billy: Yeah, sure, you're such a big shot. You think you know everything.

Helper: Well, Brandon is the best ball player in the school. You don't know what you're talking about, Billy.

Billy: Thanks a lot!

Brandon: Look, let's just play, okay? I know the rules.

Helper: Yeah, just shut up and play.

SCRIPT 2

Helper: Wow, what's going on? What's the problem?

Billy: He says you're out if the ball goes over the yellow line and I said—

Brandon: No, I didn't, you stupid liar—

Billy: Yes, you did, you jerk.

Helper: Guys, calling each other names won't help settle the problem. What are we really talking about here?

Billy: I didn't say that. I said you should be out if the ball touches the yellow line. Touching is out.

Brandon: You don't even know how to play. I've played this game before—

Billy: Yeah, sure, you're such a big shot. You think you know everything.

Helper: Look, I'm sure both of you really want to play instead of standing here arguing. Playing is more fun than arguing, right?

Billy: Yeah.

Brandon: Sure.

Helper: Okay, then what do we have to do to start playing and having fun?

RESILIENCY 4: CONFLICT SOLUTION SKILLS (3-4)
SOLVE THE CONFLICT

MAIN IDEA

Solving problems, conflicts and disagreements with words instead of with physical force promotes self-confidence and develops resiliency.

TEACHING POINTS

★ Conflict sometimes happens when people can't agree about something. Sometimes people argue or use physical force in their conflicts.

★ These are some of the essential skills we've learned about solving conflicts peacefully and without hurting one another: listen to each other; together, figure out a solution; show respect for one another; apologize; forgive; take time to cool off; ask an adult for help; know when to walk away.

MATERIALS

★ provide photographs, pictures or other images of conflict situations

LEARNING ACTIVITY: *Solve The Conflict*

1. Use pictures you have provided to discuss conflict scenarios.

2. Create a story of a conflict based on a picture. Talk the children through some essential skills of conflict solution listed in the teaching points.

DISCUSSION

1. What have we learned about how to solve conflicts?

RESILIENCY 5: ANTI-BULLYING SKILLS (3-4)
LEARNING ABOUT BULLYING

MAIN IDEA

Developing assertiveness skills helps us resist bullying and strengthen resiliency. Everyone has the right to be respected and to feel safe—in school, at home and in neighborhoods.

TEACHING POINTS

★ Bullying is threatening, frightening or harming others.

★ When we learn to recognize bullying, we can be assertive in resisting it.

★ We must tell a trusted adult when we are being bullied. Telling is different from tattling. Tattling is about getting another person into trouble. Telling is about getting help.

MATERIALS

★ none

LEARNING ACTIVITY: *Learning About Bullying*

1. Facilitate a discussion about bullying. What is a bully? Can you think of some examples of bullying? Hitting, punching, pushing or shoving a kid out of line, demanding money, taunting, name-calling, racial slur, ganging-up on a kid, spreading lies about a person, making harassing phone calls or sending threatening or frightening text messages, or excluding a kid from a group in a hurtful way.

2. What's the difference between playful teasing and hurtful bullying? Discuss the difference between harmless fun and mean-spirited, hurtful taunting.

3. No one deserves to be bullied just because she is different. We all have the right to be accepted for who we are—different looks, different abilities, different size families, and different social, cultural and religious customs.

What can you do about bullying?
  • Tell a trusted adult (teacher, parent, principal, coach). Adults care and want to help.
  • Avoid fighting. Violence doesn't solve the problem or conflict; it makes it worse.
4. • Tell the bully in a strong, confident way, "I want you to stop now." First, practice this.
  • Try to be with friends on the bus, in the cafeteria, between classes, or while walking to and from school.
  • Choose friends who are supportive and who will include you in their activities.

DISCUSSION

1. How does knowing what to do about bullying help you?

2. What is the difference between telling and tattling?

3. How would you recognize the difference between playful teasing and hurtful taunting?

CONFRONTING BULLYING

MAIN IDEA

Developing assertiveness skills helps us resist bullying and strengthen resiliency. Everyone has the right to be respected and to feel safe—in school, at home and in neighborhoods.

TEACHING POINTS

★ Bullying violates our right to be who we are.

★ When we learn to recognize bullying, we can be assertive in resisting it.

MATERIALS

★ none

LEARNING ACTIVITY: *Confronting Bullying*

1. Read one statement at a time from the list below. After reading the statement, ask: "Who is speaking: a bully, a bullied person or a bully-proofed person? How do you know?" Some answers might be: the bully sounds mean, hostile, threatening. The bullied person sounds frightened, intimidated, or maybe sad. The bully-proofed person sounds confident and strong.

2. If it's a bullied person, ask, "What can the bullied boy do to feel confident?" If it's a bully-proofed person, ask, "What is the bully-proofed person actively doing to counter bullying?" If it's the bully speaking, ask, "How could that be handled?"

The Statements:
3.
• "When I wake up in the morning, I feel like I don't want to go to school because I'm afraid I'm going to get picked on."
• "I don't like these kids who come from a foreign country, so I give them a hard time."
• "I used to walk home from school alone and this nasty kid would always ride up on his bike and make me give him my spare change. Now I feel safe walking home from school with two or three friends. The nasty kid doesn't bother me anymore."
• "In school there are two boys who always laugh at me because I don't talk good English. And then I feel so upset I can't concentrate all day."
• "This jerk is always showing off how smart he is, so I push him around. I tell him, maybe you're smart in class, but you're nothing in my school yard."
• "In the school I used to go to, they didn't do anything about the bullies. Now in this school, I see that when you tell the teachers they talk to the bully and he stops bothering the kids."
• "There's this boy on the school bus named Kevin and he always makes fun of me just because I wear thick glasses."
• "I told the boy who was always hassling me in the corridor to quit it or I would report him to the principal. And he stopped bothering me."

DISCUSSION

1. How do you feel when you hear a bully talking? When you hear a bullied kid speaking? When you hear a confident kid speaking?

2. What have we learned about confronting bullying?

RESILIENCY 5: ANTI-BULLYING SKILLS (3-4)
LETTER TO A BULLY

MAIN IDEA

Developing assertiveness skills helps us resist bullying and strengthen resiliency. Everyone has the right to be respected and to feel safe—in school, at home and in neighborhoods.

TEACHING POINTS

* Bullying violates our right to be who we are.
* When we learn to recognize bullying, we can be assertive in resisting it.
* Strengthening relationships counters the tendency toward bullying behavior and sensitizes children to one another.

MATERIALS

* paper and pencil or pen

LEARNING ACTIVITY: *Letter To A Bully*

1. Now that we have discussed bullying, use your imagination to write a letter to a bully (real or imagined). This letter is not intended to be given to the bully, but to help you practice being assertive. In your letter, tell the bully how his bullying behavior makes you feel. State that you want him to stop the bullying—and firmly state what you will do if he doesn't stop immediately.

2. Have the children read their letters. Children who are not particularly self-confident can gain courage from listening to children who are proactive. Relationships can be strengthened by generating empathy and understanding of one another.

DISCUSSION

1. What did you hear in someone else's letter that you could begin doing about bullying?

2. What else did you learn from these letters?

3. How did it help you to listen to what other kids wrote in their letters?

4. How did writing a letter to a bully help you?

POSITIVE RELATIONSHIPS

MAIN IDEA

Developing assertiveness skills helps us resist bullying and strengthen resiliency. Everyone has the right to be respected and to feel safe—in school, at home and in neighborhoods.

TEACHING POINTS

★ We can create positive relationships.
★ There should be no tolerance for bullying.

MATERIALS

★ poster board or paper and art materials

LEARNING ACTIVITY: *Positive Relationships*

1. Facilitate a discussion about what builds positive relationships (friendliness, respect, cooperation, caring, consideration, courtesy, helping) and what makes relationships negative? (bullying, hostility, disrespect). Can you think of others?

2. Create a poster that sends a message about promoting positive relationships and not tolerating bullying.

3. Have each child show her poster and briefly describe it.

DISCUSSION

1. What is a new idea you learned about positive relationships and stopping bullying?

2. What does "no tolerance" mean?

3. What does "no tolerance" for bullying mean?

RESILIENCY 5: ANTI-BULLYING SKILLS (3-4)
ARE YOU A BULLY?

MAIN IDEA

Developing assertiveness skills helps us resist bullying and strengthen resiliency. Everyone has the right to be respected and to feel safe—in school, at home and in neighborhoods.

TEACHING POINTS

★ Bullying is threatening, frightening or harming others.
★ Bullying can happen face-to-face or in other ways.
★ Cyberbullying can include sending threatening or frightening texts, e-mails, or instant messages; posting mean pictures or messages about others in blogs or on web sites.
★ When we learn to recognize bullying, we can be assertive in resisting it.
★ You can learn respectful ways to treat your friends and others.

MATERIALS

★ *Are YOU A Bully?* activity sheet

LEARNING ACTIVITY: *Are YOU A Bully?*

1. Facilitate a discussion about bullying. A lot of children have a good idea of what bullying is because they see it every day! Some examples: punching, shoving and other acts that hurt others physically. Other ways: keeping certain kids out of a group; teasing in a mean way; getting kids to "gang up" on others.

2. Tell the children there are many reasons why some kids bully others. Ask the children if any of these sound familiar: "I see others doing it." "It makes me feel, stronger, smarter, or better than the kid I'm bullying." "It's a good way to keep others from bullying me."

3. Introduce the term "cyberbullying." Ask the children if they have access to Internet social networking sites (Facebook©, MySpace©, Twitter©), email, instant messaging, or text-messaging features on a cell phone. Use the teaching points to define and discuss the concept of cyberbullying.

4. Hand out the *Are YOU A Bully?* activity sheet and ask the children to complete it. Review and discuss.

DISCUSSION

1. Why do kids bully?

2. What do you do that could be considered bullying?

3. Discuss what you learned that can help you to not bully others.

Name_____ Date_____

ARE YOU A BULLY?

Answer these questions to find out if you've ever bullied someone.
Check a box next to a statement if you've ever done these things.

☐ Whenever you see a particular kid, you tease him or her in a mean way.

☐ You often make fun of what a certain boy or girl looks like.

☐ You regularly keep another kid from eating lunch with you and your friends.

☐ You and your friends always exclude a particular kid from playing on your team.

☐ Your older brother or sister is always pushing you around and you do the same thing to another kid.

☐ You and your friends enjoy making mean prank phone calls to other kids.

If you checked any boxes, you are not alone. Kids bully other kids. Bullying is serious and it is very hurtful. It even makes some kids afraid to go to school.

We each have the power to recognize bullying
and not do it to others.

RESILIENCY 6: FRIENDSHIP SKILLS (3-4)

PERSONAL OBJECTS BAG

MAIN IDEA

Maintaining closeness, connection and support through friendships are integral components for developing resiliency. Sharing becomes a pathway to building friendships.

TEACHING POINTS

★ Sharing is foundational for building friendships.

MATERIALS

★ Children bring a bag of five personal objects that are important to them.

LEARNING ACTIVITY: *Personal Objects Bag*

1. Introduce the idea of learning about each other's interests. Children are encouraged to share some personal information about themselves.

2. Ask them to bring in a bag with any five personal objects that reveal who they are (family photo, award, favorite book, something from a collection). Give them time to present their items.

3. Encourage questions to facilitate more interest.

DISCUSSION

1. How does sharing help us to feel friendly?

2. How does knowing about someone personally build friendships?

WHAT DOES FRIENDSHIP LOOK LIKE?

MAIN IDEA

Maintaining closeness, connection and support through friendships are integral components for developing resiliency. Sharing becomes a pathway to building friendships.

TEACHING POINTS

★ Sharing is foundational for building friendships.

MATERIALS

★ scissors

★ glue sticks

★ felt pens

★ magazine clippings, Internet images, drawings

★ poster board or paper

LEARNING ACTIVITY: *What Does Friendship Look Like?*

1. Collect pictures that represent friendship. These can be photographs, magazine clippings, greetings cards, images from the Internet, and drawings. Have extra materials on hand.

2. Facilitate a discussion about how these images represent friendship. What is friendship? Some possible answers: when you and another person like being with each other, enjoy playing together, enjoy talking together, and when you feel good about the other person.

3. Divide the children into groups of three and ask them to work together to assemble a *Friendship Poster,* from the materials.

4. Display the posters. Invite each trio to explain their poster's message and meaning.

DISCUSSION

1. What did you learn about friendship by working together on this project?

2. How do we build friendships?

FRIENDSHIP STORIES

MAIN IDEA

Maintaining closeness, connection and support through friendships are integral components for developing resiliency. Sharing becomes a pathway to building friendships.

TEACHING POINTS

★ Sharing is foundational for building friendships.

★ Reading stories about friends and friendships helps children learn about the special ways in which friendships are formed and maintained.

MATERIALS

★ storybooks

LEARNING ACTIVITY: *Friendship Stories*

1. Read a story and then ask questions to facilitate a discussion. How are the characters in the story becoming friends? How do they settle their differences or problems? What kind of friendship behavior do you hear in the story?

RECOMMENDED BOOKS:
• A Rainbow of Friends by P.K. Hallinan (Nashville, TN: Ideals Publications, 2001).
• Being Friends by Karen Beaumont (New York: Penguin Putnam Books for Young Readers, 2002).
• Best Friends by Marcia Leonard (Brookfield, CT: Millbrook Press, 1999).
• Chicken Chickens by Valeri Gorbachev (New York: North-South Books, 2001).
• Clifford Makes a Friend by Norman Bridwell (New York: Scholastic, 1998).
• Duck on a Bike by David Shannon (New York: Scholastic, 2002).
• Flip & Flop by Dawn Apperley (New York: Scholastic, 2001).
• Make New Friends by Rosemary Wells (New York: Hyperion, 2002).
• Making Friends by Fred Rogers (New York: Putnam Publishing Group, 1996).
• My Best Friend Moved Away by Nancy L. Carlson (New York: Penguin Putnam Books for Young Readers, 2001).
• My Friend Bear by Jez Alborough (Cambridge, MA: Candlewick Press, 2001).
• The Best of Friends by Pirkko Vainio (New York: North-South Books, 2000).
• The Other Side by Jacqueline Woodson (New York: Penguin USA, 2001).
• The Rainbow Fish by Marcus Pfister (New York, NY: North-South Books, 2000).
• Wemberly Worried by Kevin Henkes (New York: Greenwillow Books, 2000).
• What Will I Do Without You? by Sally Grindley (New York: Scholastic, 1999).
• Where is My Friend? by Marcus Pfister (New York: North-South Books, 2001).
• Will You Be My Friend? by Nancy Tafuri (New York: Scholastic, 2000).
• Will You Forgive Me? by Sally Grindley (New York: Kingfisher, 2001).
• Witzy's Best Friends by Suzy Spafford (New York: Scholastic, 2002).

DISCUSSION

1. Explain something you learned about friendship.

2. Why is it important to have friends?

3. How would you feel if you lost a friendship?

RESILIENCY 6: FRIENDSHIP SKILLS (3-4)
FRIENDSHIP PHRASES

MAIN IDEA

Maintaining closeness, connection and support through friendships are integral components for developing resiliency. Sharing becomes a pathway to building friendships.

TEACHING POINTS

★ Friendships develop from specific behaviors.
★ Being a good friend helps two people feel good—you and your friend.

MATERIALS

★ scissors
★ glue sticks
★ felt pens

★ poster board
★ chalkboard, whiteboard or chart paper

LEARNING ACTIVITY: Friendship Phrases

1. Facilitate a discussion about acts of friendship (reaching out, making the first move). Some examples:
• Invite a kid you don't know or who is new to your school to eat lunch with you and your friends.
• Choose to play with someone you don't know.
• If someone slips and falls and is hurt, go to an adult and get help for him.
• Offer to help a new student at your school.
• Wish someone a happy birthday even if you don't know her very well.
• Congratulate a friend who receives a special award (in school or in scouting).
• If a friend is being bullied or feeling badly about something, offer to go with him to tell a trusted adult at school or at home. We all need support.
• Praise or encourage a teammate.

2. As these acts of friendship are being suggested, write them in slogan form on the board or chart paper (Friends Reach Out. Friends are Nice. Friends Show They Care. Friends Listen. Friends Invite. Friends Are Helpers. Friends Unite. Friends Are Team Players.).

3. Instruct the children to create a poster using one of these friendship phrases. Make these posters colorful and positive.

DISCUSSION

1. What have you learned about acts of friendship from these posters?

2. What is a new act of friendship you could do today?

I AM A GOOD FRIEND

MAIN IDEA

Maintaining closeness, connection and support through friendships are integral components for developing resiliency. Sharing becomes a pathway to building friendships.

TEACHING POINTS

★ Friendships develop from specific behaviors.
★ Being a good friend helps two people feel good—you and your friend.

MATERIALS

★ paper and pencil or pen

LEARNING ACTIVITY: *I Am A Good Friend*

1. Facilitate a discussion reviewing the qualities of a good friend. Refer back to the *Friendship Poster* for ideas (trusting, sharing, helping, listening, respecting, reaching out, caring).

2. Instruct the children to write a fifty-word statement expressing what makes them a good friend. "I am a good friend because……"

3. Have the children read their statements.

DISCUSSION

1. What are the qualities that make a good friend?

2. What's one of your friendship behaviors that you would like to strengthen?

GRADES 5-6 (AGES 10-12) LESSONS

INTRODUCING!

MAIN IDEA

Self-awareness is recognizing and appreciating how each of us is unique and special. This includes our personal qualities and skills, and the ways in which we grow, learn and thrive. At the same time, we learn to appreciate and respect what is distinct and similar about others. With a healthy foundation of self-awareness, resiliency can develop and grow.

TEACHING POINTS

★ Review: each person has unique physical traits and abilities.

★ A sense of self-awareness is a strong protection against peer pressure.

★ Awareness of our individuality increases resiliency.

MATERIALS

★ none

LEARNING ACTIVITY: *Introducing!*

1. Tell the children that they will do an activity that will help them feel more self-confident. Instruct them to pair up with someone they don't know. One child plays the interviewer and asks her partner to tell about herself. The interviewer can ask helpful questions about family background, place of birth, favorite activities, etc.

2. The interviewer stands behind the seated child who has just been interviewed, and says: "Introducing_____ (child's name)," and tells everyone about this child.

3. Reverse roies and repeat this activity.

DISCUSSION

1. What was it like for you to interview someone?

2. What was it like for you to talk about yourself?

3. What was it like to hear yourself introduced and talked about?

4. What kind of similarities and differences did we hear about?

MY GROWTH AND MY GOALS

MAIN IDEA

Self-awareness is recognizing and appreciating how each of us is unique and special. This includes our personal qualities and skills, and the ways in which we grow, learn and thrive. At the same time, we learn to appreciate and respect what is distinct and similar about others. With a healthy foundation of self-awareness, resiliency can develop and grow.

TEACHING POINTS

★ We have strengths and we do many things well. When new situations come along, we are challenged to develop new strengths.

★ Admitting that we need to get stronger at something means that we want to do something the best that we can.

MATERIALS

★ a current photo of each child   ★ paper and pencil or pen

LEARNING ACTIVITY: *My Growth And My Goals*

1. Tell the children they are going to write letters to themselves and then read those letters again later in the year.

2. Their letters should describe their appearances, families, favorite foods and music, who their friends are; also their favorite activities, sports and hobbies, pets, dreams or ambitions. Include their photos in the letter.

3. On the reverse side of the paper, ask the children to write at least ten goals that they would like to accomplish this year. Have them seal and address their letters and photos to themselves. Collect the letters.

4. Later in the year, return the letters to the children. Tell them that everyone develops emotionally, physically, mentally and socially in their own way. Ask them to read their letters and notice what kinds of changes they have seen in themselves.

DISCUSSION

1. What new interests have you developed?

2. What new friends have you made?

3. What is something new that you have learned?

4. Have you accomplished your goals? Some of your goals? All of your goals? What did you do to reach your goals? Who helped you reach your goals?

APPRECIATION GAME

MAIN IDEA

Self-awareness is recognizing and appreciating how each of us is unique and special. This includes our personal qualities and skills, and the ways in which we grow, learn and thrive. At the same time, we learn to appreciate and respect what is distinct and similar about others. With a healthy foundation of self-awareness, resiliency can develop and grow.

TEACHING POINTS

★ Each person has unique strengths.

★ Appreciating your strengths builds self-awareness.

MATERIALS

★ *Appreciating _____ activity sheet*

LEARNING ACTIVITY: *Appreciation Game*

1. Tell the children that today they are going to focus on strengths. What is a strength? Everyone has strengths—an exceptional capability, a special competency, a mastery, a talent. List examples on the board (friendliness, honesty, great basketball skills).

2. Hand out the activity sheet to the children and tell them to write their own names in the space next to "Appreciating____." Collect the papers.

3. Hand out one of the activity sheets to a child and say: When this paper comes to you, look at the name at the top of the page and write down a strength statement in a box and your own name in a corner of the same box. Look at the example of *Appreciating_____*. After you've written down the strength statement, hand the sheet to your neighbor. Continue handing the paper around to all the kids. Collect all the sheets when they are completed.

4. The next day, have the children read their own *Appreciating _____sheets*.

DISCUSSION

1. How does it feel to read strength statements written about you by others?

2. How did you feel writing strength statements about others?

3. Do you feel that any of your strengths were not recognized?

4. Why is it important to appreciate our own strengths and those of others?

Name_____ Date_____

RESILIENCY 1: SELF-AWARENESS SKILLS (5-6)

APPRECIATING Jennifer_____

You're good at math. *Max*		
	You are very friendly. *Jessica*	
You're sma~~rt~~ *Jas~~~~*		
		GOOD ATHLETE *Noah*
You have a great smile! *Michael*		
	GREAT FRIEND *Ashley*	
		You are fun to be with. *Kim*

Name_____ Date_____

RESILIENCY 1: SELF-AWARENESS SKILLS (5-6)

APPRECIATING _____

I HAVE A DREAM

MAIN IDEA

Self-awareness is recognizing and appreciating how each of us is unique and special. This includes our personal qualities and skills, and the ways in which we grow, learn and thrive. At the same time, we learn to appreciate and respect what is distinct and similar about others. With a healthy foundation of self-awareness, resiliency can develop and grow.

TEACHING POINTS

★ Making us aware of, and giving voice to, our personal dreams, ambitions, values and goals strengthens our sense of individuality.

★ When we are influenced by peer pressure to "fit in," we diminish our individuality and uniqueness. A sense of self-awareness is a strong protection against peer pressure.

★ Awareness of our individuality increases resiliency.

MATERIALS

★ paper and colored pencils

LEARNING ACTIVITY: *I Have A Dream*

1. Ask the children to write a paragraph about a special hope, dream, ambition or goal. On the reverse side of the paper, draw a picture of what this would look like.

2. Invite them to read their paragraphs and show their drawings. Encourage everyone to validate and affirm each reader with positive expressions ("Sounds great," "Well written," "Good luck," "You can do it!").

DISCUSSION

1. What have you learned about your hopes, dreams, ambitions?

2. What have you learned about your friends' dream, hopes, etc?

I AM!

MAIN IDEA

Self-awareness is recognizing and appreciating how each of us is unique and special. This includes our personal qualities and skills, and the ways in which we grow, learn and thrive. At the same time, we learn to appreciate and respect what is distinct and similar about others. With a healthy foundation of self-awareness, resiliency can develop and grow.

TEACHING POINTS

★ Making us aware of, and giving voice to, our personal dreams, ambitions, values and goals strengthens our sense of individuality.

★ When we are influenced by peer pressure to "fit in" we diminish our individuality and uniqueness. A sense of self-awareness is a strong protection against peer pressure.

★ Awareness of our individuality increases resiliency.

MATERIALS

★ large poster paper
★ magazines

★ scissors
★ markers, glue sticks, pens and pencils

LEARNING ACTIVITY: *I Am!*

1. Have the children create an "I Am" collage. Include in it what they enjoy doing, people they admire, activities they enjoy, or anything else that presents a picture of themselves. Have them write their names on the other side of the poster.

2. Display the completed posters and then have the children guess which collage belongs to whom and explain why they made that guess.

DISCUSSION

1. What clues did you see in each collage that helped you guess its owner?

2. What have you learned about your friends?

3. What have you learned about yourself?

RESILIENCY 1: Self-Awareness Skills (5-6)

PERSONAL BEST

MAIN IDEA

Self-awareness is recognizing and appreciating how each of us is unique and special. This includes our personal qualities and skills, and the ways in which we grow, learn and thrive. At the same time, we learn to appreciate and respect what is distinct and similar about others. With a healthy foundation of self-awareness, resiliency can develop and grow.

TEACHING POINTS

★ Making us aware of, and giving voice to, our personal qualities and strengths develops our self-awareness.

★ Awareness of our individuality increases resiliency.

MATERIALS

★ paper and pencil or pen

LEARNING ACTIVITY: *Personal Best*

1. Instruct the children to take a sheet of paper and tear it into ten strips. On each strip, have them write a personal quality or strength.

2. Say, "Consider giving up one of these personal qualities. Remove that strip from your list and place it aside. Now, give up another. What kind of person are you without those two qualities or strengths?" Continue until they have eliminated six of these.

DISCUSSION

1. What would you be like without these personal qualities?

2. How complete or incomplete do you feel without one or two or more of them?

3. How important is each personal characteristic to your sense of identity?

4. What have you learned about yourselves from looking very closely at the personal characteristics that make up your unique identity?

A VOCABULARY OF FEELINGS

MAIN IDEA

Expression of emotions, especially positive emotions, using a vocabulary of "feeling words" builds resiliency. Positive emotions influence a resilient response to adversity. ·

TEACHING POINTS

★ Our emotions—feelings—are what make us human. Feelings are neither right nor wrong. Feelings are personal, yet everyone experiences similar kinds of feelings.

★ When we identify our own feelings, we are better able to communicate with others.

★ We are so wonderfully alive and responsive to what's going on in our lives that we can have several different feelings in a day.

MATERIALS

★ paper and pencil or pen

★ *A Vocabulary of Feelings* Word List handout

★ dictionary and thesaurus

LEARNING ACTIVITY: *A Vocabulary of Feelings*

1. Distribute copies of the *A Vocabulary of Feelings* handout.

2. Ask the children to choose six feeling words they do not already know. Have them use a thesaurus and a dictionary to look up definitions, synonyms and antonyms for the six feeling words they chose.

3. Ask them to write a sentence for each of their six feeling words. Have the children share their sentences.

DISCUSSION

1. What are some advantages of having a vocabulary of feeling words?

2. What new feeling words did you learn today?

A VOCABULARY OF FEELINGS

angry	troubled	annoyed	disappointed	cranky
furious	ticked off	upset	hostile	wary
scared	concerned	amused	hurt	thrilled
glad	excited	pleased	content	awful
lonely	put-down	embarrassed	hopeless	helpless
sorrowful	powerless	useless	unworthy	foolish
awkward	silly	humiliated	happy	nervous
puzzled	shocked	relieved	depressed	anxious
timid	ashamed	suspicious	worried	jittery
uneasy	afraid	confused	frustrated	miserable
elated	calm	pleased	sad	jealous
hopeful	surprised	disgusted	guilty	proud

HANDLING MY ANGER

MAIN IDEA

Expression of emotions, especially positive emotions, using a vocabulary of "feeling words" builds resiliency. Positive emotions influence a resilient response to adversity.

TEACHING POINTS

★ Our emotions—feelings—are what make us human. Feelings are neither right nor wrong.
★ Feelings are personal, yet everyone experiences similar kinds of feelings. We should never be ashamed of our feelings.
★ Sometimes we may feel strong emotions, such as anger. Understanding our anger and developing appropriate ways to manage it develops resiliency.

MATERIALS

★ *Appropriate Ways I Handle My Anger* activity sheet
★ chalkboard, whiteboard or chart paper

LEARNING ACTIVITY: *Handling My Anger*

1. Begin by writing "anger" on the board or chart paper and ask, "Has anyone felt this emotion today? Yesterday? What happened? Briefly write these down. For example: a kid tripped me and I got up and shoved him. Gather other examples.

Emphasize and discuss the following points about anger:
• Anger is a basic human emotion.
2. • There are inappropriate and destructive ways of expressing anger and there are appropriate ways of expressing anger.

3. Go over the examples of inappropriate responses and brainstorm appropriate ways of dealing with them using: S-I-T, nonviolent language, assertiveness, S-T-O-P, apologizing, Compile a list of the appropriate ways of handling anger and write each on the board.

4. Hand out the activity sheets. From the list you made, have children write three anger situations and responses using the appropriate ways of handling their anger.

5. Ask them to share their anger situations and in what new, appropriate ways they would handle anger.

DISCUSSION

1. How does it feel to have a way out of being stuck in anger?

2. How does it feel to know you are in charge of your feelings and actions?

3. What kind of school, family or neighborhood would we have if people just stayed angry and expressed their anger destructively?

4. What would it be like to have a school, family or neighborhood where we have appropriate ways of handling anger?

Name_____ Date_____

APPROPRIATE WAYS I HANDLE MY ANGER

List three situations that make you angry. Next to each, write an appropriate way to handle that situation.

ANGER SITUATIONS	APPROPRIATE WAYS TO HANDLE THE SITUATIONS
1. _____ _____ _____ _____	**1.** _____ _____ _____ _____
2. _____ _____ _____ _____	**2.** _____ _____ _____ _____
3. _____ _____ _____ _____	**3.** _____ _____ _____ _____

RESILIENCY 2: EMOTIONAL SKILLS (5-6)
EXPRESSING EMOTIONS

MAIN IDEA

Expression of emotions, especially positive emotions, using a vocabulary of "feeling words" builds resiliency. Positive emotions influence a resilient response to adversity.

TEACHING POINTS

★ Our emotions—feelings—are what make us human. Feelings are neither right nor wrong.
★ Feelings are personal, yet everyone experiences similar kinds of feelings. We should never be ashamed of our feelings.
★ Sometimes we may feel strong emotions, such as anger. Understanding our anger and developing appropriate ways to manage it develops resiliency.

MATERIALS

★ poster board or paper and decorating materials

LEARNING ACTIVITY: *Expressing Emotions*

1. Have children create engaging posters that send a message of how to express strong emotions appropriately. Display the posters.

DISCUSSION

1. Why is it important to express your strong emotions appropriately?

2. What are "appropriate" responses?

RESILIENCY 2: EMOTIONAL SKILLS (5-6)

WHAT WOULD YOU DO?

MAIN IDEA

Expression of emotions, especially positive emotions, using a vocabulary of "feeling words" builds resiliency. Positive emotions influence a resilient response to adversity.

TEACHING POINTS

★ Our emotions—feelings—are what make us human. Feelings are neither right nor wrong.

★ Feelings are personal, yet everyone experiences similar kinds of feelings. We should never be ashamed of our feelings.

★ Sometimes we may feel strong emotions like anger. Understanding our anger and developing appropriate ways to manage it develops resiliency.

MATERIALS

★ paper and pencil or pen

LEARNING ACTIVITY: *What Would You Do?*

1. Introduce the following situations to the children:
• You overhear your friends talking about an upcoming event (party, ball game, amusement park) to which you are not invited.
• Your parents get angry with you for letting your room become a total disaster zone.

2. Ask the children, "What feelings might you have? What would you think or want to say—and to whom?" Facilitate a discussion.

3. Role-play the same situation, but expressing yourself in an appropriate way. Have the children write down three different situations (from their own experiences) and how they would respond in an appropriate way.

DISCUSSION

1. What did you have to consider to make your responses appropriate?

2. What would it be like to have a school, family or neighborhood where we all have appropriate ways of handling anger?

CONVERSATION COURTESY

MAIN IDEA

Communication skills are essential in everyday life. Communication is how we give or receive information. Communication can be verbal or non-verbal. Strengthening communication skills builds resiliency for coping with many different situations.

TEACHING POINTS

★ Courteous speaking and courteous listening are essential to positive, productive communication.

MATERIALS

★ chalkboard, whiteboard or chart paper
★ *Courteous Listening and Speaking Skills* activity sheet

LEARNING ACTIVITY: *Conversation Courtesy*

1. Ask the children to name some "listening courtesy" skills and make a list on the board or chart paper. Include: look directly at the speaker; don't interrupt; show you are listening by nodding or by making comments; focus—don't let your attention wander; allow speaker to finish; ask your questions after the speaker finishes; be courteous; acknowledge the speaker. Say: "I understand what you are saying." Or: "I also think that…."

2. Ask the children to name some "speaking courtesy" skills and and make a list on the board or chart paper. Include: think about what you want to say before you speak; be sure to have the listener's attention before speaking; look directly at the listener; speak clearly; avoid monotone; show respect to your listener; speak up so you can be heard; use polite words; stay on topic; use phrases such as "My point is…."

3. Instruct the children to pair-up and have a conversation. Tell them to pay attention to their speaking and listening skills as they talk.

4. Have them complete the activity sheet by writing about two "listening courtesy" and two "speaking courtesy" skills and situations.

DISCUSSION

1. Which skills were you aware of using when listening and speaking?

2. How effective were you at using these skills?

3. What skills could you strengthen?

4. What skills did you notice your partner using?

Name_____ Date_____

COURTEOUS LISTENING AND SPEAKING SKILLS

1. Write down a **listening** courtesy skill that you would like to practice:

_____

Write down an imaginary situation describing how you use this skill:

_____

_____

_____

2. Write down a **listening** courtesy skill that you would like to practice:

_____

Write down an imaginary situation describing how you use this skill:

_____

_____

_____

3. Write down a **speaking** courtesy skill that you would like to practice:

_____

Write down an imaginary situation describing how you use this skill:

_____

_____

_____

4. Write down a **speaking** courtesy skill that you would like to practice:

_____

Write down an imaginary situation describing how you use this skill:

_____

_____

CALLING 9-1-1

MAIN IDEA

Communication skills are essential in everyday life. Communication is how we give or receive information. Communication can be verbal or non-verbal. Strengthening communication skills builds resiliency for coping with many different situations.

TEACHING POINTS

★ Communication is using words effectively to give or receive information or messages.
★ Communication can be face-to-face, in writing or on the telephone.
★ There are many reasons why we communicate: sometimes to connect with our friends; sometimes to give information. Sometimes we communicate to ask for help from adults for others or ourselves in situations that involve health and safety. It could be at school and it could also be at home.

MATERIALS

★ chalkboard, whiteboard or chart paper
★ *Teaching Your Child How To Use 9-1-1* handout for parents

LEARNING ACTIVITY: *Calling 9-1-1*

1. Tell the children that you are going to review how they should communicate on the telephone when dialing 9-1-1 to ask for help in an emergency.

2. Review when to call 9-1-1: in an emergency when an adult is not present. What is an emergency? A fire; someone is seriously hurt or unconscious; someone is trying to break into the home.

3. Review what is not an emergency (lost pet, sprained ankle or stolen bicycle). Teach that if the child is in doubt he/she should call 9-1-1. It is better to be safe than sorry. Don't ever call 9-1-1 as a joke.

4. What do you say to 9-1-1? Say, "I need help." Then listen carefully for their questions. What's your address? Where do you live? What is your emergency? What's the problem? Who needs help? Is the person awake and breathing? Is the person bleeding? It's okay to trust the 9-1-1 operator and give him/her your personal information.

5. It's okay to be frightened in an emergency, but it's also important to stay calm and speak slowly, clearly and loudly.

6. Do not hang up. The operator will stay on the phone with you until help arrives.

7. Have the children role-play calling 9-1-1 with an adult playing the 9-1-1 operator. Instruct them to be supportive of others' efforts.

DISCUSSION

1. Have you or anyone you know ever called 9-1-1? What happened?

2. What is the job of a 9-1-1 operator? What other kinds of emergency workers are found in your community? What do they do?

3. Would you like to be a 9-1-1 emergency worker someday—or another kind of emergency helper in your community? Why?

TEACHING YOUR CHILD HOW TO USE 9-1-1

from the health experts of Nemours

One of the challenges you have as a parent is to help your child acquire the skills to work through whatever obstacles life presents. Teaching your child how to use 911 in an emergency could be one of the simplest - and most important - lessons you'll ever share.

Talking About 9-1-1 With Your Child

Not that many years ago, there was a separate telephone number for each type of emergency agency. For a fire, you called the fire department number. For a crime, you called the police. For a medical situation, you phoned the ambulance or doctor.

In 1968, the U.S. government worked with the phone company to establish 9-1-1 as a central number for all types of emergencies. An emergency dispatch operator quickly takes information from the caller and puts the caller in direct contact with whatever emergency personnel are needed, thus making response time quicker.

According to the National Emergency Number Association, 9-1-1 covers nearly all of the population of the United States. Check your phone book to ensure that 9-1-1 is the emergency number you should use in your area.

Everyone needs to know about calling 9-1-1 in an emergency. But children in particular need specifics about what an emergency is. Asking your child, "What would you do if we had a fire in our house?" or "What would you do if you saw someone trying to break in?" gives you a chance to discuss what constitutes an emergency and what should be done if one occurs. Role playing is an especially good way to address various emergency scenarios and give your child the confidence he or she will need to handle them.

For younger children, it might also help to talk about who the emergency workers are in your community - police officers, firefighters, paramedics, doctors, nurses, and so on - and what kinds of things they do to help people who are in trouble. This will paint a clear picture for your little one of not only what types of emergencies can occur, but also who can help.

When to Call 9-1-1

Learning what is an emergency goes hand in hand with learning what isn't. A fire, an intruder in the home, an unconscious family member - these are all things that would require a call to 9-1-1. A skinned knee, a stolen bicycle, or a lost pet wouldn't. Still, teach your child that if ever in doubt and there's no adult around to ask to always make the call. It's much better to be safe than sorry.

Make sure your child understands that calling 9-1-1 as a joke is a crime in many places. In some cities, officials estimate that as much as 75% of the calls made to 9-1-1 are nonemergency calls. These are not all pranks. Some people accidentally push the emergency button on their cell phones. Others don't realize that 9-1-1 is for true emergencies only. That means it's not for such things as a flat tire or even about a theft that occurred the week before.

Stress to your child that whenever an unnecessary call is made to 9-1-1, it can delay a response to someone who actually needs it. Most areas now have what is called enhanced 9-1-1, which enables a call to be traced to the location from which it was made. So if someone dials 9-1-1 as a prank, emergency personnel could be dispatched directly to that location. Not only could this mean life or death for someone having a real emergency on the other side of town, it also means that it's very likely the prank caller will be caught and punished.

How to Use 9-1-1

Although most 9-1-1 calls are now traced, it's still important for your child to have your street address and phone number memorized. Your child will need to give that information to the operator as a confirmation so time isn't lost sending emergency workers to the wrong address.

Make sure your child knows that even though he or she shouldn't give personal information to strangers, it's OK to trust the 911 operator. Walk him or her through some of the questions the operator will ask, including:
- Where are you calling from? (Where do you live?)
- What type of emergency is this?
- Who needs help?
- Is the person awake and breathing?

RESILIENCY 3: COMMUNICATION SKILLS (5-6)

Explain to your child that it's OK to be frightened in an emergency, but that it's important to stay calm, speak slowly and clearly, and give as much detail to the 9-1-1 operator as possible. If your child is old enough to understand, also explain that the emergency dispatcher may give first-aid instructions before emergency workers arrive at the scene.

Make it clear that your child should **not** hang up until the person on the other end says it's OK, otherwise important instructions or information could be missed.

More Safety Tips

Here are some additional safety tips to keep in mind:

* Always refer to the emergency number as "nine-one-one" not "nine-eleven." In an emergency, your child may not know how to dial the number correctly because of trying to find the "eleven" button on the phone.

* Make sure your house number is clearly visible from the street so that police, fire, or ambulance workers can easily locate your address.

* If you live in an apartment building, make sure your child knows the apartment number and floor you live on.

* Keep a list of emergency phone numbers handy near each phone for your children or babysitter. This should include police, fire, and medical numbers (this is particularly important if you live in one of the few areas where 911 is not in effect), as well as a number where you can be reached, such as your cell phone, pager, or work number. In the confusion of an emergency, calling from a printed list is simpler than looking in the phone book or figuring out which is the correct speed-dial number. The list should also include known allergies, especially to any medication, medical conditions, and insurance information.

* If you have special circumstances in your house, such as an elderly grandparent or a person with a heart condition, epilepsy, or diabetes living in your home, prepare your child by discussing specific emergencies that could occur and how to spot them.

* Keep a first-aid kit handy and make sure your child and babysitters know where to find it. When your child is old enough, teach him or her basic first aid.

This information was provided by KidsHealth, one of the largest resources online for medically reviewed health information written for parents, kids, and teens. For more articles like this one, visit KidsHealth.org or TeensHealth.org. © 1995-2008. The Nemours Foundation. All rights reserved.

- - - - - - - - - - - - - - ✂   Cut along the dotted line.   ✂ - - - - - - - - - - - - - -

EMERGENCY INFORMATION CARD

Fill out all the information that applies to your family and post near the telephone.
Teach your child where it is and how to read the information.

My name is _____

My mother's/father's/guardian's (circle one) name is _____

My mother's/father's/guardian's (circle one) name is _____

My street address is _____ Apartment number _____

City _____Zip Code _____

My nearest cross streets are _____

My house phone number is _____

My mother's/father's/guardian's phone number is _____

My family members have the following allergies/medical conditions/medications

_____

RESILIENCY 3: COMMUNICATION SKILLS (5-6)

CONVERSATION BREAKERS AND MAKERS

MAIN IDEA

Communication skills are essential in everyday life. Communication is how we give or receive information. Communication can be verbal or non-verbal. Strengthening communication skills builds resiliency for coping with many different situations.

TEACHING POINTS

★ Conversation Breakers are like red lights—they stop conversations.
★ Conversation Makers are like green lights—they keep messages flowing in a conversation.
★ Effective conversation needs Conversation Makers.

MATERIALS

★ chalkboard, whiteboard or chart paper
★ *Conversation Breakers and Conversation Makers* activity sheet

LEARNING ACTIVITY: *Conversation Breakers and Makers*

1. Brainstorm some Conversation Breakers and write them on the board or chart paper.
• Ridicule: "That's a stupid thing to say." "Ha, ha, you're so lame ."
• Character Attack: "You're dumb." "You sound like an idiot."
• Dominating: "I want it done my way." "No, no—I said NO!"
• Threatening: "If you do, I'll tell on you."
• Sarcasm: "Don't you ever do anything right?"
• Angry Shouting: "SHUT UP!"

2. Now ask for examples of Conversation Makers and write them on the board or chart paper.
• Inviting: "Tell me more." "What else?"
• Accepting: "I think that's fine—I understand."
• Interested: "That's great."
• Repeating: "So, it's really important for you to be in the chess club."
• Supportive: "I agree that you should go to the party."
• Honest: "It's not a good idea to lie to her."

3. Hand out the activity sheet, *Conversation Breakers and Conversation Makers* and have the children complete it. Review and discuss their answers.

DISCUSSION

1. Is it difficult to tell the difference between a *Conversation Breaker and Conversation Maker*? Why or why not?

2. Why is it important to use Conversation Makers?

Name_____ Date_____

CONVERSATION BREAKERS AND MAKERS

Directions: Next to each sentence, write "B" if it's a conversation BREAKER or "M" if it's a conversation MAKER.

1. "That's a really interesting point." _____

2. "I don't really care what you say." _____

3. "That's the stupidest thing I've ever heard." _____

4. "Tell me about your trip to the amusement park." _____

5. "Your grandma sounds like a nice lady." _____

6. "You could have done better if you weren't so lazy." _____

7. "I think you'll have a nice time at her party." _____

8. "You're right—your hair does look stupid." _____

9. "I agree—that's a good solution." _____

10. "Hey, what happened on the field trip?" _____

11. "You're such a complainer." _____

12. "Hey, that's great—you got an "A" on your book report." _____

13. "That's lame." _____

14. "Just shut up." _____

15. "Your jokes are always funny." _____

RESILIENCY 3: COMMUNICATION SKILLS (5-6)

TURNING BREAKERS INTO MAKERS

MAIN IDEA

Communication skills are essential in everyday life. Communication is how we give or receive information. Communication can be verbal or non-verbal. Strengthening communication skills builds resiliency for coping with many different situations.

TEACHING POINTS

★ Conversation Breakers are like red lights—they stop conversations.
★ Conversation Makers are like green lights—they keep messages flowing in a conversation.
★ Effective conversation needs Conversation Makers.

MATERIALS

★ *Turning Conversation Breakers Into Makers* activity sheet

LEARNING ACTIVITY: *Turning Breakers Into Makers*

1. Say, "Listen to this sentence and the Conversation Breaker that follows. Let's brainstorm a Conversation Maker instead."
  • "I can't do this math homework—it's too hard."
      • Breaker: "Quit complaining and just do your work."
      • Maker: "I'll help you—let's try doing it together."
  • "I feel like such an idiot—I don't get what he was talking about."
      • Breaker: "You're a space case—try listening for a change."
      • Maker: _____
  • "Tiffany, I'm sorry I teased you in front of the other kids."
      • Breaker: "Thanks a lot" (sarcastically).
      • Maker: _____
  • "I wish I was invited to Chloe's party."
      • Breaker: "Oh forget it—you know she doesn't like you."
      • Maker: _____

2. Hand out the *Turning Conversation Breakers Into Makers* activity sheet and ask the children to complete it.

DISCUSSION

1. What's involved in changing a Conversation Breaker into a Conversation Maker?

2. What's valuable to you about this exercise?

Name_____   Date_____

RESILIENCY 3: COMMUNICATION SKILLS (5-6)

TURNING BREAKERS INTO MAKERS

Instructions: Read each numbered sentence. Then read its conversation breaker. Notice how it stops further conversation. Write down a conversation maker that helps continue the conversation. Think about being positive, accepting, supportive, understanding, and honest.

EXAMPLE: "I don't want to go to the art museum—that's a stupid field trip."
Breaker: "What a whining complainer you are."
Maker: "Give it a chance—it could be fun."

1. "My dad's such a jerk—he won't let me go with you Friday night."
Breaker: "Yeah, he's an even bigger jerk than my dad."
Maker:_____.

2. "Let's invite that new kid in class to sit with us at lunch."
Breaker: "That's dumb. Don't you see what a geek he is?"
Maker:_____.

3. "I don't want to help wash the dishes tonight."
Breaker: "You're just lazy."
Maker:_____.

4. "This is too much math homework—I'm not doing it."
Breaker: "Just shut up and do it."
Maker:_____.

5. "I'm sorry—it was an accident—I didn't mean to run into you."
Breaker: "Pay attention—watch where you're walking."
Maker:_____.

6. "I can't believe you're saying that about her—she's so nice."
Breaker: "Ah, you don't know anything."
Maker:_____.

7. "Hey, can I help you with that?"
Breaker: "Leave me alone—don't bother me."
Maker: _____.

8. "My brother told me to stay out of the ocean because it's polluted."
Breaker: "Your brother doesn't know what he's talking about."
Maker: _____.

RESILIENCY 3: COMMUNICATION SKILLS (5-6)

"I" MESSAGES

MAIN IDEA

Communication skills are essential in everyday life. Communication is how we give or receive information. Communication can be verbal or non-verbal. Strengthening communication skills builds resiliency for coping with many different situations.

TEACHING POINTS

★ Review: We use the "I" message to communicate firmly without blaming or being mean.
★ The "I" message helps us to be assertive—it's how we stand up for ourselves. The "I" message is a strong, clear, confident statement about our needs, ideas and feelings.
★ We use the "I" message to communicate in an appropriate way when we feel upset.
★ The "You" message is not an appropriate way to communicate when there's a problem or when we are upset or angry. The "You" message blames the other person and can make a situation worse.
★ The "I want" sentence expresses what you want to happen to change the situation.

MATERIALS

★ chalkboard, whiteboard or chart paper
★ "I" Messages activity sheet

LEARNING ACTIVITY: "I" Messages

1. Here is the two-sentence "I" message. Write on board or chart paper:
• I feel_____(say your feeling) when you_____(describe the person's action because_____ (say why the action effects you). I want_____(what you need to improve the situation).

Use the two-sentence "I" message for these situations:
• EXAMPLE: You loaned your bike to Tyler so he could go home and get his baseball glove. When he returned you noticed that the front fender was bent and the light was cracked. You ask him "What happened?" He answers "Nothing, what's your problem?"

2.
• "I" message: "Tyler, I feel angry when you break my bike and ignore me because now I have to fix it myself. I want you to take responsibility and get my bike fixed."
• EXAMPLE: Your little brother makes a mess of the bedroom you share. Your mother gets home, takes one look at the room, and immediately blames you.
• "I" message: "Mom, I feel frustrated when you blame me because I'm getting scolded for something I didn't do. I need you to ask me what happened."

3. Working in groups of three, complete the two-sentence "I" message activity sheet.

DISCUSSION

1. Describe how your group worked together to come up with the "I" messages.

2. What was difficult about it? What was easy about it?

Name_____ Date_____

"I" MESSAGES

Instructions: Write an "I" message for each situation.

1. You want to work on a special school project with a friend, but he tells you, "Forget it—I've already asked some other kids."

_____

_____

2. A friend at school is having a birthday party over the weekend. You tell your best friend that you haven't been invited and he laughs and makes fun of you.

_____

_____

3. You let a friend wear your favorite tee shirt and she returns it torn. When you ask about it, she gets annoyed and says, "Liar—you gave it to me that way."

_____

_____

4. You find out that a classmate is saying mean things about you to other kids.

_____

_____

5. A friend promises to eat lunch with you at school, but then goes off with other kids at lunchtime leaving you alone.

_____

_____

6. You're standing in line and two kids are roughhousing. They bump into you making you drop your books and your poster project. Both get stepped on and dirty.

_____

_____

CONFLICT SOLUTION FORMULA

MAIN IDEA

Solving problems, conflicts and disagreements with words instead of with physical force promotes self-confidence and develops resiliency.

TEACHING POINTS

★ A conflict is when people can't agree about something. Sometimes people argue or use physical force in their conflict.

★ Using words is a peaceful way to solve conflict.

MATERIALS

★ chalkboard, whiteboard or chart paper

LEARNING ACTIVITY: *Conflict Solution Formula*

1. Write the following conflict solution formula on the board or chart paper:
> **A = ASK** what the problem is.
> **B = BRAINSTORM** solutions that are positive.
> **C = CHOOSE** a solution that is fair to all.
> **D = DO** try the solution. Make the effort.
> **E = EVALUATE** whether it worked for you and the other person.

2. Review the formula with the children. Emphasize that the goal is to solve the conflict peacefully. When it comes to brainstorming solutions, here are some possibilities: listen to each other; show respect for one another; apologize; forgive; take time to cool off; ask for help; know when to walk away, etc. Brainstorm positive solutions.

3. Now ask the children for examples of conflict and have them practice using the conflict solution formula.

DISCUSSION

1. How does using the formula (like using a tool) help you solve a conflict?

2. What can you do if your first "solution" doesn't solve the conflict?

3. Why is it important for conflict solutions to be positive?

WHY FIGHTING FAILS

MAIN IDEA

Solving problems, conflicts and disagreements with words instead of with physical force promotes self-confidence and develops resiliency.

TEACHING POINTS

★ Fighting sometimes gets people what they want, so they believe that fighting works.

★ Fighting, however, has destructive consequences.

MATERIALS

★ none

LEARNING ACTIVITY: *Why Fighting Fails*

1. Facilitate a discussion using the following questions:
• Why do people sometimes end up fighting to settle their conflicts?
• Have you had a physical confrontation? Describe what happened.
• What are the negative consequences of fighting or using violence to settle conflicts?
• What could be the consequences of fighting at home? At school? At the park?

2. Now that we have discussed the consequences of fighting to settle a conflict, what are more appropriate ways to settle a conflict?

DISCUSSION

1. How do you feel to know that you can settle a conflict peacefully? Discuss.

2. What else did you learn about settling conflicts peacefully?

PEACE AREA

MAIN IDEA

Solving problems, conflicts and disagreements with words instead of with physical force promotes self-confidence and develops resiliency.

TEACHING POINTS

★ A conflict is when people can't agree about something. Sometimes people argue or use physical force in their conflict.

★ Conflicts can be resolved more easily in a pre-designated "peace area."

MATERIALS

★ none

LEARNING ACTIVITY: *Peace Area*

1. Introduce a permanent place for conflict solution called a "peace area." Moving to an area away from the initial conflict may help to defuse emotions and allow children to concentrate on the process of solving the problem.

2. Ask about a recent conflict. Invite the children involved to go to the designated peace area to use the problem-solving skills already taught: listen calmly to each other; figure out a solution together; say I'm sorry; forgive; ask an adult for help; take turns; flip a coin; take time to cool off; show respect; know when to walk away.

DISCUSSION

1. How does it feel to be able to solve a conflict peacefully?

2. Discuss how using the "peace area" helps.

RESILIENCY 4: CONFLICT SOLUTION SKILLS (5-6)
SOLVING A CONFLICT

MAIN IDEA

Solving problems, conflicts and disagreements with words instead of with physical force promotes self-confidence and develops resiliency.

TEACHING POINTS

★ A conflict is when people can't agree about something. Sometimes people argue or use physical force in their conflict.

★ There are essential skills for solving conflicts peacefully and without hurting one another: listen to each other; together, figure out a solution; show respect for one another; apologize; forgive; take time to cool off; ask an adult for help; know when to walk away.

MATERIALS

★ provide photographs, pictures and images

LEARNING ACTIVITY: *Solving A Conflict*

1. Use pictures you've prepared to discuss conflict scenarios. Create a story of a conflict based on the picture. Talk the children through some essential skills of problem solving. For example, show a picture of a sad and unhappy boy. Say, "This is Jared. He wanted to play baseball after school, but the other kids didn't choose him for their teams. What is the problem? What do you think Jared could do?" Children could brainstorm the following solutions for Jared to try (ask the boys again if he could play with them, find someone else to play with or ask an adult for help).

2. Use another picture and repeat Step 1.

DISCUSSION

1. What have we learned about how to solve a conflict?

2. How does it feel to know you can make something that feels bad feel better?

RESILIENCY 4: CONFLICT SOLUTION SKILLS (5-6)
USING THE A-B-C-D-E FORMULA

MAIN IDEA

Solving problems, conflicts and disagreements with words instead of with physical force promotes self-confidence and develops resiliency.

TEACHING POINTS

★ A conflict is when people can't agree about something. Sometimes people argue or use physical force in their conflict.

★ Using words is a peaceful way to solve conflict.

MATERIALS

★ *Script for Conflict about Using a PlayStation*

LEARNING ACTIVITY: *Using The A-B-C-D-E Formula*

1. Re-introduce the five-step conflict-solving formula.
A = ASK "What's the problem?"
B = BRAINSTORM solutions that are positive
C = CHOOSE a solution that is fair to all
D = DO try the solution. Make the effort.
E = EVALUATE whether it worked for you and the other person.

2. Invite two volunteers to role-play a scripted conflict over a PlayStation. Instruct the other children to watch and listen carefully and be thinking about the *A-B-C-D-E* formula.

3. After the role-playing, brainstorm how to apply the *A-B-C-D-E* formula. You may role-play several of the suggestions. Ask, "What might happen if….(you did this or that)?"

4. Now, instruct the children to work in small groups. Have them write their own conflict scenario and how to apply the *A-B-C-D-E* formula. They can role-play these to the others.

DISCUSSION

1. What can we say or do to stop a conflict situation and try to solve it?

2. Tell us about one of your conflict situations. How did you solve at the time? How would you solve it now?

Name_____ Date_____

SCRIPT FOR CONFLICT RESOLUTION

Child 1: Wants to use the PlayStation

Child 2: Is using the PlayStation

Child 1: Hey, can you get off the PlayStation? I just got this new game and I want to play it now

Child 2: But I'm playing my favorite game. I'm about to level up!

Child 1: So! I need to get online now so I can play with my friends.

Child 2: Okay! Sounds good! Can I play, too?

Child 1: No, we already have an equal number of people. There's no room for you on a team.

Child 2: Whatever! I'm using it now, so forget it.

Child 1: Don't be a jerk! You can play that game any time.

Child 2: I get that, but I really want to play my game now!

Child 1: So do I.

Child 2: Whatever jerk! You're so lame.

Child 1: I'm telling on you!

Child 2: Fine! I'm telling on you too!

RESILIENCY 4: CONFLICT SOLUTION SKILLS (5-6)
NAME THOSE SKILLS

MAIN IDEA

Solving problems, conflicts and disagreements with words instead of with physical force promotes self-confidence and develops resiliency.

TEACHING POINTS

★ A conflict is when people can't agree about something. Sometimes people argue or use physical force in their conflict.

★ These are some of the essential skills we've learned about solving conflicts peacefully and without hurting one another: listen to each other; together, figure out a solution; show respect for one another; apologize; forgive; take time to cool off; ask an adult for help; know when to walk away.

MATERIALS

★ provide photographs, pictures or other images of conflict situations

★ paper and pencil or pen

LEARNING ACTIVITY: *Name Those Skills*

1. Display the pictures of conflict solutions and have the students discuss what they see. Talk them through the essential skills of problem solving listed in the teaching points.

2. Have the children each select a picture of a conflict and write a paragraph describing how they would use one of the peaceful conflict solutions skills to solve the conflict.

DISCUSSION

1. What have we learned about how to solve a conflict?

2. How does it feel to know you can make something that feels bad feel better?

NO BULLYING

MAIN IDEA

Developing assertiveness skills helps us resist bullying and strengthen resiliency. Everyone has the right to be respected and to feel safe—in school, at home and in neighborhoods.

TEACHING POINTS

★ Bullying is when someone threatens, hurts or frightens us.

★ When we learn to recognize bullying, we can be assertive in resisting it.

★ We can tell a trusted adult. Telling is different from tattling. Telling is about getting help. Tattling is about getting another person into trouble.

MATERIALS

★ chalkboard, whiteboard or chart paper

LEARNING ACTIVITY: *No Bullying*

1. Facilitate a discussion about bullying. Almost anyone—kids and adults—can be bullied
• Are you being bullied? Have you been bullied? Have you seen other kids being bullied?
• How does bullying make you feel? Angry? Overpowered? Weak? Ashamed? Afraid to tell someone about it?

2. Brainstorm with the children. Write down their responses on a No Bullying Chart on the chalk board or chart paper. What are some things they can do about bullying?
• Tell a trusted adult —someone you can talk to who will listen and help. Too afraid or ashamed to tell? Then have a friend go with you to the adult. Don't keep it a secret. Adults care and want to help you when they hear about bullying. Reporting is not "tattling." It's the right thing to do.
• Stay in a group. Bullies like to victimize kids who are alone. This is less likely to happen if you're hanging out or playing with other kids.
• Be assertive. Stand tall. Use a strong voice, and name the bullying behavior that you want stopped. "Cut it out! Stop teasing me!" Walk away. Be sure to tell an adult.
• Ignore it. Bullies enjoy it when their teasing upsets their victims. Some suggestions: walk away without looking at them or look completely uninterested.
• Join clubs and take part in other activities where you are likely to make new friends with kids who share your interests.
• Remember that you are not to blame for being targeted by a bully. It is not your fault. Nobody deserves to be hurt or threatened or bullied.
• Don't start skipping class or avoiding school or not going places you enjoy out of fear of meeting the bully. You have the right to go anywhere!
• Don't hurt yourself. Some kids get so upset and sad about being bullied, or feel so helpless and hopeless, that they may try to hurt themselves. This is not an answer to the problem. Tell an adult, and get help.

DISCUSSION

1. What skills have you already been using?

2. What new skills do you feel confident trying?

3. What new skills do you need to practice?

RESILIENCY 5: ANTI-BULLYING SKILLS (5-6)
DO YOU BULLY?

MAIN IDEA

Developing assertiveness skills helps us resist bullying and strengthen resiliency. Everyone has the right to be respected and to feel safe—in school, at home and in neighborhoods.

TEACHING POINTS

★ Bullying is when someone threatens, hurts or frightens us.

★ Cyberbullying can include sending nasty texts, emails, instant messages, or posting nasty pictures or messages about others in blogs or on web sites.

★ When we learn to recognize bullying, we can be assertive in resisting it.

★ There are many effective skills and strategies for resisting bullying.

★ You can learn better ways to treat your friends and others.

MATERIALS

★ *Do You Bully?* activity sheet

LEARNING ACTIVITY: *Do You Bully?*

1. Facilitate a discussion about bullying. A lot of children have a good idea of what bullying is because they see it every day! Bullying happens when a child intimidates another child. Some examples: punching, shoving and other acts that hurt others physically. Other ways: spreading rumors; keeping certain kids out of a group; teasing in a mean way; getting kids to "gang up" on others.

2. There are many reasons why some children bully others. Ask the children if any of these sound familiar: "I see others doing it." "It's what you do if you want to hang out with the right crowd." "It makes me feel, stronger, smarter, or better than the kid I'm bullying." "It's a good way to keep others from bullying me."

3. Review the concept of cyberbullying. Ask the children if they have access to Internet social networking sites (Facebook©, MySpace©, Twitter©), email, instant messaging, or text-messaging features on a cell phone. Use the teaching points to define and discuss the concept of cyberbullying.

4. Hand out the *Do You Bully?* activity sheet and ask the children to complete it. Review and discuss their responses.

DISCUSSION

1. Why do kids bully?

2. What do you do that could be considered bullying?

3. What have you learned that can help you to not bully others?

Name_____ Date_____

DO YOU BULLY?

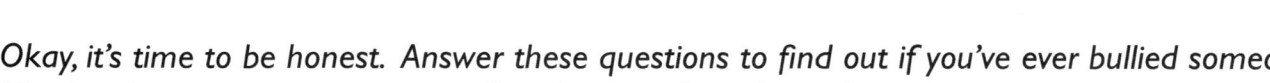

Okay, it's time to be honest. Answer these questions to find out if you've ever bullied someo
Check a box next to a statement if you've ever done these things.

☐ There is a boy or girl who you repeatedly pick on in a mean way just because you feel like it.

☐ You ask someone else to threaten another kid you don't like.

☐ You spread a rumor about another kid, in a note, e-mail or through a conversation or instant messaging.

☐ There is a particular kid that you see often, and tease in a mean way.

☐ Repeatedly, you make fun of a kid's physical appearance.

☐ You do mean things in order to earn the approval of and to be accepted by a certain group of kids.

☐ You and your friends have regularly prevented another kid from hanging out or playing or eating lunch with you.

☐ You pulled a prank you thought would be funny only to see a kid feel badly.

☐ Whenever you need cash you force other kids to give you spare change.

☐ You are picked on and in turn you get even by picking on others.

If you checked any of these boxes, you are not alone. All over our country, in all kinds of schools and neighborhoods, kids bully other kids. Bullying is serious and it is very hurtful. It causes the victimized kids to feel badly and even do poorly in school.

It doesn't have to be this way. You can learn about better ways to treat other kids you know.
You can become part of the solution to putting an end to bullying.

Bullying is something we all need to think about. Whether we've done it ourselves...or whether friends or other kids we know are doing it...we all need to recognize that bullying has painful consequences. It may not be happening to you today, but it could tomorrow. Working together, we can make everyone's lives happier and safer.

POSITIVE RELATIONSHIPS

MAIN IDEA

Developing assertiveness skills helps us resist bullying and strengthen resiliency. Everyone has the right to be respected and to feel safe—in school, at home and in neighborhoods.

TEACHING POINTS

★ We can create positive relationships.
★ There should be no tolerance for bullying.

MATERIALS

★ poster boards or paper and art materials

LEARNING ACTIVITY: *Positive Relationships*

1. Facilitate a discussion about positive relationships. What builds positive relationships? Friendliness, respect, cooperation, caring, consideration, courtesy, helping.

2. What makes relationships negative? Bullying, hostility, disrespect, etc. Ask the children if they can think of other examples.

3. Instruct the children to create a poster that promotes positive relationships and a no tolerance for bullying.

4. Have each child show his or her poster and briefly explain it.

DISCUSSION

1. What new ideas did you learn about putting an end to bullying?

2. What new ideas did you learn about building positive relationships?

PROTECTION AGAINST CYBERBULLYING

MAIN IDEA

Developing assertiveness skills helps us resist bullying and strengthen resiliency. Everyone has the right to be respected and to feel safe—in school, at home and in neighborhoods.

TEACHING POINTS

★ Cyberbullying is using the electronic media—emails, text messages, IM's, the internet and cell phones—anonymously and repeatedly to intimidate or humiliate someone.

★ There should be zero tolerance for bullying, including cyberbullying.

★ Use all electronic technology responsibly.

MATERIALS

★ none

LEARNING ACTIVITY: *Protection Against Cyberbullying*

1.
Have a discussion about cyberbullying.
What is cyberbullying?
• It can be "bashing"—ridiculing you.
• It can be a threat on your life—"You're dead meat! I know where you live."
• It can be someone spreading lies about you in text or images on a web site.
• It can be hate messages—"I hate you. Everyone at school hates you."
• It can be posting something vulgar or obscene on your web site guest book.
• It can be someone pretending to be friendly and tricking you to reveal information about yourself and then posting that information on another web site. Even if the bullying turns out to be a "prank" it is still ugly and scary.

2.
Why do kids do it?
• Some kids do it to torment others to feel more powerful.
• Some do it for laughs or to get a reaction.
• Some do it because they are bored and have too many tech toys available.
• Others may start out defending themselves from a bully and find out that they enjoy getting revenge.

3.
Protect yourself against cyberbullies.
• Don't cooperate with cyberbullies by forwarding their hateful messages about others.
• Don't be a bystander and allow your friends and others to be cyberbullied.
• Suppose you receive an online message that makes you angry? Don't use your computer as a weapon by responding with a hateful message of your own. Get away from the computer. Go for a run, shoot some hoops, or call a friend on the phone. When you're calm again you won't feel like striking out at anyone and behaving like a cyberbully.
• Always send messages that are respectful of others.

DISCUSSION

1. How does understanding cyberbullying help you use technology more responsibly?

2. What are some other ways to protect yourself and others from cyberbullying?

RESILIENCY 6: FRIENDSHIP SKILLS (5-6)
FRIENDSHIP POSTERS

MAIN IDEA

Maintaining closeness, connection and support through friendships are integral components for developing resiliency. Sharing becomes a pathway to building friendships.

TEACHING POINTS

★ Sharing is foundational for friendship building

MATERIALS

★ scissors
★ glue sticks
★ felt pens

★ magazine clippings, Internet images, drawings
★ poster board or paper

LEARNING ACTIVITY: *Friendship Posters*

1. Ask the children to bring in images that depict friendship. These can be photographs, magazine clippings, greeting cards, images from the Internet, and drawings. Have extra materials on hand.

2. Facilitate a discussion: How do these images represent friendship? What is friendship? Some possible answers: when you and another person like being with each other, enjoy playing together, or enjoy talking together; when you feel good about the other person; when you trust, share, listen, say good things about each other to others.

3. In a group of three, work together to assemble a *Friendship Poster* from the materials.

4. Display the posters and invite each group to explain their poster's message and meaning to the others.

DISCUSSION

1. What did you lean about friendship by working together on this project?

2. How do we make a friend?

3. Why does it take time and effort to develop a friendship?

RESILIENCY 6: FRIENDSHIP SKILLS (5-6)
FRIENDSHIP STORY

MAIN IDEA

Maintaining closeness, connection and support through friendships are integral components for developing resiliency. Sharing becomes a pathway to building friendships.

TEACHING POINTS

★ Sharing, trust and loyalty are the foundations for friendship.

★ Friendships involve how we feel, what we think and how we behave toward others. Good friendships enrich our lives.

MATERIALS

★ paper and pencil or pen

LEARNING ACTIVITY: *Friendship Story*

1. Ask the children to each write a one-page story that expresses their ideas about friendship. It can be about something that really happened to them or they can make up a story. Tell them to write the story so that it teaches others something about friendship. When finished, have the children read their stories.

DISCUSSION

1. What have we learned about friendship from these stories?

RESILIENCY 6: FRIENDSHIP SKILLS (5-6)

FRIENDS AND FRIENDSHIP

MAIN IDEA

Maintaining closeness, connection and support through friendships are integral components for developing resiliency. Sharing becomes a pathway to building friendships.

TEACHING POINTS

★ Sharing, trust and loyalty are the foundations for friendship.

★ Friendships involve how we feel, what we think and how we behave toward others. Good friendships enrich our lives.

★ Friendships are often easy and natural. At other times, friendships may be tested by challenging situations.

★ Healthy friendships have healthy boundaries.

MATERIALS

★ *Friends and Friendship* activity sheet

LEARNING ACTIVITY: *Friends And Friendship*

1. Facilitate a discussion about friendship:
• How is a friend different from an acquaintance?
• What makes a "best friend" different from other friends?
• What would you do or say if your friend did something dishonest or mean?
• If you did something dishonest or mean, what would you want a friend to do or say?
• Are there special circumstances when someone might need to break a confidence or a promise he has made to a friend?
• What would you expect from a friend if something embarrassing happened to you?
• Are there limits on loyalty in a friendship?
• Can a friend be much older or much younger than you? Here, you can choose an age differential to facilitate a discussion of peer-to-peer friendships and inappropriate friendships.
• What could end a friendship?

2. Now hand out the *Friends and Friendship* activity sheet and have the children answer the questions.

DISCUSSION

1. What have we learned about friendship?

2. What do we mean by "boundaries" in friendships? What purpose do they serve in a friendship?

Name_____ Date_____RESILIENCY

FRIENDS AND FRIENDSHIP

1. How is a friend different from an acquaintance?

_____

_____

2. What makes a "best friend" different from other friends?

_____

_____

3. What would you do or say if your friend did something dishonest or mean?

_____

_____

4. If you did something dishonest or mean, what would you want a friend to do or say?

_____

_____

5. Are there special circumstances when someone might need to break a confidence or a promise he has made to a friend?

_____

_____

6. What would you expect from a friend if something embarrassing happened to you?

_____

_____

7. Are there limits on loyalty in a friendship? If so, what are they?

_____

_____

8. Can a friend be much older or younger than you? If so, how is this friendship different?

_____

_____

9. What could end a friendship?

_____

_____

ACTS OF FRIENDSHIP

MAIN IDEA

Maintaining closeness, connection and support through friendships are integral components for developing resiliency. Sharing becomes a pathway to building friendships.

TEACHING POINTS

★ Friendships develop from specific behaviors.

★ Being a good friend helps two people feel good—you and your friend.

MATERIALS

★ poster boards or paper and art materials

LEARNING ACTIVITY: *Acts of Friendship*

1. Guide a discussion about "Acts of Friendship." Focus on motivating children to go beyond talking about friendship to actually extending acts of friendship. The emphasis is on personal acts of reaching out, making the first move, etc.

You can use the slogan, "Let's move from knowing what to do, to doing what we know!" Some examples:
- Invite a kid you don't know or who is new to your school to join you and your friends at your lunch table.
- Choose to play with a boy or girl you don't know.
- Choose someone you don't know or a child new to the school to be on your side in a game at recess.
- Offer someone new help to find their way to the cafeteria or principal's office, and go with them.

2.
- If a child is ill and missing school, call them on the phone with some friendly greeting. Let someone know they are missed and cared about.
- If you learn that today is someone's birthday, wish them happy birthday even if you don't know them very well. It's their special day to receive some extra attention. Your smile and friendly actions are a special gift.
- Congratulate someone who has received an award for doing something good.
- If a friend is being bullied, offer to go with him to tell a trusted adult at school or home. People need support sometimes.
- Actively praise or encourage a teammate.

3. As the ideas are being suggested, write them in slogan form on the board (Friends Reach Out. Friends Show They Care. Friends Listen. Friends Invite! Friends Unite! Friends Are Team Players!)

4. Instruct the children to create posters with friendship slogans. Make these posters colorful and positive. Display the posters and invite everyone to look at them.

DISCUSSION

1. What have we learned today about acts of friendship?

2. What have you learned about friendship from these posters?

BUILDING FRIENDSHIPS

MAIN IDEA

Maintaining closeness, connection and support through friendships are integral components for developing resiliency. Sharing becomes a pathway to building friendships.

TEACHING POINTS

★ Sharing is foundational for friendship building.

★ Friendships involve how we feel, what we think and how we behave toward others. Good friendships enrich our lives.

MATERIALS

★ Children bring a bag of five personal items.

LEARNING ACTIVITY: *Personal Items Bag*

1. Introduce the idea of learning about each other's interests and families. Ask the children to each bring in a bag with five personal items that symbolize or reveal something about who he/she is (a family photo, an award, a favorite book, something from a collection) to be presented the next time you meet.

2. Give the children time (perhaps two minutes each) to present their items. Encourage the children to share some personal information about themselves in connection with the items they brought.

3. Encourage questions to facilitate more personal interest.

DISCUSSION

1. How does sharing help us to feel friendly?

2. How does knowing about someone personally build friendship?

REFERENCES

Baruch, Rhoda, Grotberg, Edith, H., and Stutman, Suzanne. *Creative Anger: Putting That Powerful Emotion to Good Use.* New York: Praeger, 2007.

Brooks, Robert, Goldstein, Sam and Poulter, Stephan, B. *Raising Resilient Children: Fostering Strength, Hope, and Optimism in Your Child.* New York: McGraw-Hill Professional, 2002

Gardner, Howard. *Multiple Intelligences: The Theory in Practice.* New York: Basic Books, 1993.

Gardner, Howard. *Intelligence Reframed: Multiple Intelligences for the 21st Century.* New York: Basic Books, 1999.

Goldstein, Sam and Brooks, Robert B. *Handbook of Resilience in Children.* New York : Kluwer Academic/ Plenum Publishers, 2005.

Goldstein, Sam and Brooks, Robert B. *Understanding and Managing Children's Classroom Behavior: Creating Sustainable, Resilient Classrooms.* Hoboken: J. Wiley & Sons, 2007.

Goleman, Daniel. *Working With Emotional Intelligence.* New York: Bantam Books, 2000.

Grotberg, Edith, H. *A Guide to Promoting Resilience in Children: Strengthening the Human Spirit.* The Netherlands: Bernard van Leer Foundation, 1995.

Grotberg, Edith, H. *Resilience for Today: Gaining Strength from Adversity.* New York: Praeger, 2003.

Joseph, Joanne. *The Resilient Child: Preparing Today's Youth for Tomorrow's World.* New York: Da Capo Press, 2001.

Lee, Chris. *Preventing Bullying in Schools: A Guide for Teachers and Other Professionals.* United Kingdom: Paul Chapman Press, 2004.

Ludwig, Trudi. *My Secret Bully.* Berkeley: Tricycle Press, 2005.

Ludwig, Trudi and Gustavson, Adam. *Just Kidding.* Berkeley: Tricycle Press, 2006.

Parsons, Les. *Bullied Teacher, Bullied Student: How to Recognize the Bullying Culture in Your School and What to Do About It.* Ontario: Pembroke Publishers, 2005.

Scaglione, Joanne and Scaglione Arrica Rose. *Bully-Proofing Children: A Practical, Hands-On Guide to Stop Bullying.* Lanham: Rowman & Littlefield Education, 2006.

Sullivan, Keith. *The Anti-bullying Handbook.* Oxford: Oxford University Press, 2000.

Wolin, Stephen and Wolin, Sylvia. *The Resilient Self.* New York: Random House, 1993.

ABOUT THE AUTHORS

Pam Farkas, L.C.S.W., is a prominent educator and psychotherapist. As the Executive Director of the Dr. Jordan M. Farkas Foundation, she works with teachers, mental health professionals, parents, students and organizations. Her Hope and Help educational program has increased awareness of at-risk youth and emphasizes the positive factors that empower children to enjoy healthy fulfilling lives. Pam serves on the advisory board of the Didi Hirsch Community Mental Health Center and the American Foundation for Suicide Prevention.

Jerry Binder, Ph.D., is a social science researcher, author and distinguished educator. He presents information from research in lifespan growth and development in programs that address vital mental health concerns for adults and children. He has been a dedicated advocate for youth, beginning his career at the Hathaway-Demille Children's Village and later consulting to the Economic and Youth Opportunities Agency in Los Angeles. Dr. Binder teaches at several educational venues and consults to a number of organizations.

Barrie Richter, B.A., a graduate of UCLA, is an experienced elementary school teacher. She is a recipient of the Milken Family Award for Distinguished Educators and is a member of the National Science Teachers Association. She is dedicated to teaching children how to cope effectively with social pressures and challenges.

Illustrations by Vanessa Lindstrom, Los Angeles, CA

Layout and design by Tom Freeland, Nyack, NY

And a special thank you and much appreciation to Amber Lucille Boyd of Elevated Consulting in Philadelphia, PA who devoted countless hours of creativity, guidance and heartfelt enthusiasm in seeing our manuscript transformed into this book.

Made in the USA
Charleston, SC
13 December 2011